praise for

Embracing the Real World
The Black Woman's Guide to Life After College

"Embracing the Real World: The Black Woman's Guide to Life After College is interesting, well written, and packed with practical information for anyone entering the job market. I highly recommend the book as a great read."
—Dr. JoAnn Haysbert, President, Langston University

"Sometimes a book comes along that makes you say, 'I wish I had written that!' Embracing the Real World: The Black Woman's Guide to Life After College is a great book for all young women—regardless of race, creed, or ethnicity."
—Dianne Boardley Suber, President, Saint Augustine's College

"Embracing the Real World: The Black Woman's Guide to Life After College is a comprehensive guide that is easy to read and easy to follow with excellent discussion and examples. I highly recommend this book to every African-American woman before she first enters the job market."
—Dr. L'esa Guilian, Director of Diversity & Human Resources at California Institute of Integral Studies

"Every black woman attempting to make the most of that hard-earned college degree should read Embracing the Real World: The Black Woman's Guide to Life After College. This book is informative, thought-provoking and a pure joy to read."
—Dionne Anglin, Reporter, KDFW Fox 4 News

"*Chaz Kyser's book is a must-read for women aspiring for leadership.*"
—Dr. Shirley A.R Lewis, President, Paine College

"*Women in general and African-American women in particular face a plethora of challenges when they enter the world of work. In her book, Embracing the Real World: The Black Woman's Guide to Life After College, Chaz Kyser presents many of the issues that African-American women face, particularly in corporate America, and she provides the 'nuts and bolts' on how to negotiate through the maze to accomplish one's desired results. By using personal experiences she provides case examples of the challenges and rewards associated with a career. All college women will find useful suggestions and strategies in this book for having a meaningful career and life once they leave the academy.*"
—Dr. Elaine Johnson Copeland, President, Clinton Junior College

"*Embracing the Real World: The Black Woman's Guide to Life After College is engaging, informative and thought-provoking—not just for the recent college grad, but for those of us who are still navigating our way through the muck and mire of Corporate America. I wholeheartedly applaud Chaz Kyser and her work, and encourage every professional black woman to buy and read this book.*"
—Sharon Chandler, President, Dallas/Ft.Worth chapter of Swing Phi Swing Social Fellowship, Inc.

"*Many students have no idea of the inequalities they will face in the world of work when they graduate from college. This is especially true for black women who face a multitude of prejudices in the workplace. This book serves as an enlightening guide that provides valuable insights for black women as they enter the workplace. It also recommends ways to successfully navigate through the snares and pitfalls of a biased world.*"
—Dr. Vivian Presley, President, Coahoma Community College

Embracing the Real World
The Black Woman's Guide to Life After College

Chaz Kyser

Seshet Press

Copyright © 2006 Chaz Kyser

All rights reserved. No part of this publication may be reproduced, stored in a retrieval system, or transmitted in any form by any means—electronic, mechanical, photocopying, recording, or otherwise, without written permission from the publisher.

To make requests for excerpts or quotes send an email to info@embracingtherealworld.com.

ISBN: 0-9788188-0-6
Library of Congress Control Number: 2006907202

Cover design by Jeff Greenwood: www.jgreenwood.com
Author photo by De'Shawn Saffold

Published by Seshet Press
Printed in the United States of America
First Edition

Dedication

To seven friends and fellow graduates
of Texas State University-San Marcos: Shiloh Davis,
Yamilet Medina-Lopez, Tasha Talton, Lisa Lewis Daniels,
Edith Hardison, Robin Mitchell and Courtney Hargrove.

"To struggle and battle and overcome and absolutely defeat every
force designed against us is the only way to achieve."
—Nannie Burroughs, civil rights activist

Table of Contents

Acknowledgements — xi
Preface — xiii
Introduction — 3

Part 1: Preparing for the Real World
1. Mapping Out Your Future — 5
2. Job Search Smarts — 11
3. Applying for Positions — 17
4. Preparing for the Interview — 21
5. Twenty Pointers to a Better Interview — 33
6. Learning From Rejection — 39
7. Finding and Keeping a Career Mentor — 43
8. Staying Positive — 47

Part 2: Succeeding in the Real World
9. Letting Go of Real World Myths — 51
10. Evaluating Job Offers — 55
11. Understanding Company Benefits — 59

12.	Choosing Between Jobs	65
13.	Getting the Salary You Deserve	69
14.	Meeting & Exceeding Your Employer's Expectations	81
15.	Fitting In as the New Girl	85
16.	Building & Maintaining a Positive Image	89
17.	Managing Your Boss	97
18.	Handling Conflicts With Co-workers	107
19.	Working Around Office Politics	123
20.	Working in Corporate America	127
21.	Networking Effectively	135
22.	Losing Your Job Without Losing Yourself	139

Part 3: Real World Questions

23.	Where Should I Live?	151
24.	Why Do I Have to Pay My Dues?	157
25.	Should I Quit My Job?	161
26.	Do I Have to Get a Second Job?	169
27.	Do I Have to Go Back to School?	171
28.	Where Are My Friends?	175
29.	Is This It?	179

Part 4: Handling Real World Barriers

30.	Handling Racial Discrimination in the Workplace	183
31.	Handling Sex Discrimination & Sexual Harassment in the Workplace	189
32.	Handling the Naysayers	201
33.	Handling Self-doubt & the Fear of Failure	205

Part 5: Banking in the Real World

34. Real World Budgeting — 213
35. Reducing Post-College Debt — 223

Part 6: Real World Stories

36. Yvonne Chase on Doing It Your Way — 231
37. Jean Thompson on Getting Out of a Rut — 237
38. Talia Nye Kief on Checking Your Problems at the Door — 244
39. Angelene Hall on the Loss of Camaraderie Among African-Americans in the Professional Workplace — 246
40. Vickie Stokes on Expecting the Unexpected — 250
41. Regina Burns on Chasing Away Those Pink Slip Blues — 253
42. Darcelle Whitaker on Working in Corporate America — 256
43. Francina Harris on Deciding Who You Are Before Deciding What You Will Do — 259
44. Kalin Thomas on Travel, the Ultimate Education — 264
45. Kimberly Taylor on Defeating Discrimination at Work — 267
46. Marshawn Evans on Choosing to be Bitter or Better — 270
47. Lola Brown on Grad School Journeys: 12 Rounds to Victory — 272

48. Mavis Gragg on Finding Yourself
    in Unexpected Places   279

The ABC's of Embracing the Real World   285
Resource Guide   291
About the Author & Book Ordering Information   301

Acknowledgements

I could not have completed and published this book, nor found the courage to pursue my aspirations, if I had not been blessed with an abundance of encouraging and uplifting family, friends, co-workers and students.

I am particularly grateful to my sister, Cameron Foster-Kyser, for letting me read and re-read parts of chapters and simple sentences to her via phone over and over again at all hours of the day, and for assisting me in some way with every aspect of the book. I promise to be as helpful and encouraging when you begin working on your book, Cam—hint, hint.

Special thanks to Charlie Kyser, Caryl Foster, Ramona Crayton, Nicole Thomas, Harold Johnson, Dexter Gabriel, Rahim Rasul, Paul Munson, James Hilliard, Johnetta Jackson, Donna Barnes, Amy Love, Gary Rice, Michael Jaye Jackson, David Freeman, Trenell Miller, Antoinette Baugh, Yvonne Chase, Courtney Hargrove, Lasana Hotep, David Seats, and Louis M. McClinton. They all helped make the book better in their own way, and helped make me a better person in their own way as well.

Some people I barely knew showed an inordinate amount of enthusiasm for the book, and freely gave their advice and support. Author and career expert Beatryce Nivens allowed me to become her website's career columnist and gave me great advice worth charging for. Kathleen Domenig, publisher of Strata Publishing, Inc., graciously responded to my emails asking her about various book design questions. Sharon Chandler's positive feedback and willingness to let me speak at her organization's national Swing Phi Swing Conference is greatly appreciated. When I finally met Lisa Burrell after exchanging emails for three years she was even more nice and encouraging in person. She also gave me the perfect last sentence for one of my chapters.

Thank you Divona Phillips and Tiffany Taylor for proofreading/copyediting my book. I hope it helps land you both a job (anyone needing a good reporter or copyeditor please call me for these two brilliant women's info).

My former students—Jessica Lowe, Shaunna Cooper, Tatyana Johnson, Shamia Jackson, Kevono Hunt and Dwan Brumfield—provided an enormous amount of encouragement and sound advice. Thank you.

And finally, thank you Ted and Rhonda Pruitt for hiring me to work at your newspaper at the age of 16, and then to manage it at 21. I will always be grateful to you both for giving me my first "real" job, and taking me under your collective wings.

Preface

"Each of us should make the most of our lives. We should give life our best. Let us use our lives more wisely to choose our dreams, find our true purpose, and be as happy and successful as possible."
—Malcolm X

Embracing the Real World: The Black Woman's Guide to Life After College was begun during a very challenging period in my life. I began writing the book while working as the managing editor of a black weekly newspaper in Houston. I was 21, fresh out of college, ambitious, hopeful, and thrilled at having a job many recent college graduates would forfeit their degree for. Unfortunately, I was also very naïve.

After working in my first professional position I began to see that life in the real world was not what I had expected. What's more, no one had truly prepared me for it. I felt like I was the butt of a joke on a *Punked* episode nearly every week. After struggling with conflicts with my co-workers and boss, the demands of my job, and the stress of living on my own, I began to feel disillusioned and slightly depressed. Later experiences of job loss and the frustrations of job searching only made matters worse. Like many recent college graduates my transition from college to the working world proved to be quite difficult. And I believe being an African-American woman made the transition even more complicated.

I wrote the majority of the chapters you'll find in the book after I went through the issues they focus on, thus the book was written to help me make sense of my life as well as to help other black women make sense of theirs.

This book is filled with all the great advice that career-related books should have, based on my experiences, those of other college graduates, the insight of employers, and tons of research. You'll get schooled on everything from applying and interviewing for jobs, choosing where to live, succeeding in a new position, handling conflicts with co-workers, managing your boss, networking effectively, budgeting, negotiating your salary, and coping with job loss. But what sets this book apart from others on the market is that it's specifically written for black women and covers topics that most career-related books ignore. Handling racial and sex discrimination in the workplace, working in corporate America, building and maintaining a positive image, and handling self-doubt and the fear of failure are just a few of the chapters you'll discover in *Embracing the Real World*. And then there are the personal stories from successful women who have already walked in your shoes. They share their trials and tribulations, as well as their accomplishments and what they've learned since being handed that sacred degree.

Like everything else in life, writing this book was a great balancing act. I wanted to paint the world that you've entered as welcoming, gratifying, and full of unending opportunities, yet I knew there was more to the real world than that. So I strived to be just as realistic as I was idealistic because the truth is that college graduates of all ethnicities face a world that can be frustratingly unfair, with more obstacles than we ever imagined.

I believe I've painted a picture of both worlds. I hope you appreciate the book more because of this. Perhaps you'll even discover, as I have, that this realm called the real world is full of hard knocks but very happy endings.

Part 1
Preparing for the Real World

Introduction: Breaking New Ground

"We are the first generation of black people in 400 years who can live our dreams."
—Susan Taylor

Attaining your degree may not seem like such a big feat, but it is. According to the U.S. Census Bureau's most recent data, only 17.6 percent of African-Americans have completed four or more years of college. A lack of support, motivation, funds or ability held others back. And although there is no limit to what anyone can accomplish, the truth is that educated Americans of all ethnicities fair much better than those without a degree.

You are blessed because there has never been a better time in American history for black women with a college education. As our graduation rates have increased, so has the number of us entering fields that have primarily been comprised of men, taking management roles that would have been nearly impossible to secure decades ago, heading major subsidiaries of Fortune 500 companies, and owning our own businesses. As part of a younger generation of black women, you will help determine whether we continue to make such significant gains as these. We need more black female computer programmers, physicians, scientists, journalists, elected officials, accountants, and the like. Furthermore, we need more black women to be in positions of leadership and power at the companies they join.

Understand the enormous potential you have. Believe that you can accomplish all of your goals. Racism, sexism, fear, low self-esteem, lack of support, poverty, and all those other obstacles to people's achievement haven't stopped you thus far. There is no reason why anything or anyone should deter you now.

The times spent daydreaming and talking about what you were going to do with your life after graduation is over. It's now time to show and prove. And everyone wants to know what you're going to do now, so what are you going to tell them? More important, what are you going to tell yourself? That there are too many obstacles in the way of your success? That you don't have what it takes to accomplish your goals? That you'll just focus on getting by and try to be happy? Our ancestors would be angered by such mediocrity.

There is more than enough room in the world for you and it's time you began claiming your space. It's time for you to learn more about yourself, and find out that you're a stronger, smarter, and braver person than you ever thought possible. It's time for you to find and create opportunities for yourself and others. It's time for you to start making the world a better place in any and every way you can. It's time for you to break new ground. Make our ancestors proud.

Chapter 1

Mapping Out Your Future

> "Create a definite plan for carrying out your desire
> and begin at once, whether you're ready or not,
> to put this plan into action."
> —Napoleon Hill

As a beginning freshman you may have worked with a counselor on what is commonly called a degree plan. This plan stated the degree you were trying to achieve, outlined the classes needed to receive that degree, and then gave you a time line indicating how long it would take before you could don a cap and gown.

Now, you may have followed your plan to the letter. Or perhaps, if you were like me, you had to adjust it a couple of times. If you were very indecisive you might have changed your plan frequently, and ended up adding a couple of more semesters to your college experience. But what matters is that you graduated. You would still be in a classroom, however, if you had never had that degree plan mapping your way in and out of college.

With the start of a new phase of your life a new plan is needed. This plan will map out what will hopefully be an exciting and rewarding career, thus we'll call it your Career Plan.

Besides mapping out your future, your Career Plan will also help keep you focused. Sometimes we forget exactly what our goals are and the reasons why we chose these goals. Having something written down can reassure us that we're heading in the right direction, and remind us why we're working so hard.

The Career Plan you make for yourself should answer four basic questions:
1. *What* are my career goals?
2. *Why* have I set these goals?
3. *How* will I achieve these goals?
4. *When* should I reasonably be able to achieve these goals?

What are my career goals?

This part of your plan will state the goal(s) you want to reach in your career. This can be as simple as stating what title you want to hold, such as an African-American history professor, or an accountant for one of the nation's leading accounting firms.

If you have two very different career goals, like you want to be a public relations director and a clothing designer, then you would need to make a Career Plan for both goals. It's okay if you're unsure about exactly what position you hope to hold, but know what field you want to work in. For example, instead of writing that you want to be a dentist, you could put that you want to work in dentistry. However, the more specific you are the more helpful your Career Plan will be.

Why have I set these goals?

This part of your plan will explain why you've set your stated career goals. The explanation should be straightforward. For example: I am going to be an African-American history professor because (1) I love sharing knowledge about African-American history, (2) professors get paid well, are respected, have a high level of autonomy, and a flexible work schedule, (3) I want to work in academia, (4) I know I'll be a great professor.

How will I achieve these goals?

This part of the plan explains what you have to accomplish to achieve your goal(s) step-by-step. Research on your desired profession may be needed to fill this section out. If you wanted to be a college professor, for example, then talking to your former professors and researching various graduate programs would be desirable.

Once you've done your research you should be able to write out a general path you have to follow. For example, you might write: In order to be an African-American history professor I have to:

1. Attend school full-time to receive my Master's in History.

2. Attend school full-time to receive my Ph.D. in African-American Studies.

—Become noted for my own research and work in the field.

—Network with other professors, especially at schools with an African-American Studies department.

3. Work on my dissertation.

4. Receive my Ph.D. and then apply for a full-time teaching position within a university that has a respected African-American Studies department.

When should I reasonably be able to achieve these goals?

The biggest question is almost always "when?" Answering the when question will help keep you on track once you decide what you're focused on becoming. The word "reasonably" is inserted into that question so that you'll set a realistic time line. Setting deadlines in your time line that are close to impossible to meet will discourage you when they aren't met. On the other hand, setting deadlines that are too easy to meet will keep you from working hard and going as far as you can in your career.

The time line you make will be based off of what you wrote down in "How will I achieve these goals?" For each step you wrote down you should give a maximum amount of time allotted to get past that step and on to the next one. Research will definitely be needed to determine how long each step should take. Some steps will be taken simultaneously and should be written as such. The following is a sample time line:

CAREER TIME LINE

- Get my Master's in History. *—2 Years*
- Work on my Ph.D. in African-American Studies. *— 3 Years*
- Complete my dissertation and Ph.D. *—1 Year*
- Find a position as an African-American history professor. *—1 Year*

Estimated time to working as an African-American history professor: *7 Years*

Your time line may have to be adjusted due to unforeseeable circumstances that happen down the road. Or you might find shortcuts to reaching your career goal(s) or have to take additional steps. What's important is that you have a plan to follow.

Once you have your career ambitions mapped out, you can start working toward securing your goals. In the case of someone who aspires to be a professor, most of the person's energy will be spent completing further studies to secure a position. However, people wanting to snag non-academic positions and move up in their careers are more likely to need adequate work experience before they need another degree. The next two chapters focus on getting the position you desire so you can begin gaining the experience needed to excel in your career.

Sample Career Plan

WHAT are my career goals?
To work as an African-American history professor at a university with a respected African-American Studies department.

WHY have I set these goals?
- I love sharing knowledge about African-American history.
- College professors get paid fairly well, are respected, have a high level of autonomy, and a flexible work schedule.
- I want to work in academia.
- I know I'll be a great professor.

HOW will I achieve these goals?
- By attending school full-time to receive my Master's in History.
- By attending school full-time to receive my Ph.D. in African-American Studies.
- By becoming noted for my own research in the field.
- By networking with other professors, especially those at universities with an African-American Studies department.
- By applying for a full-time teaching position with a university with an established African-American Studies department.

WHEN should I reasonably be able to achieve my goals?
- Get my Master's in History. —2 Years
- Work on my Ph.D. in African-American Studies. — 3 Years
- Work on my dissertation. —1 Year
- Receive my Ph.D and find a position at a respected university as an African-American history professor. —1 Year

Estimated time to reach my career goal: 7 years

Chapter 2

Job Search Smarts

"Perseverance is a great element of success; if you only knock long enough and loud enough at the gate you are sure to wake up somebody."
—Henry Wadsworth Longfellow

It would be terrific if every degree came along with a job we loved, but then we wouldn't be living in the "real world." In the real world a great job is a prized possession, and what's more, it's something that the average college graduate has to work hard to get. According to the National Center for Education Statistics, nearly 1.5 million bachelor's degrees are conferred every year in America. Roughly all college graduates look for some type of employment upon graduation, which means you have some pretty tough competition.

I thought I was going to have a nervous breakdown when I started applying for jobs after I lost a managing editor position one year after graduation. My ego shrunk to the size of a penny when weeks went by and not one person I sent a resume to called me back. "Don't they know how smart I am?" I thought. "I have two degrees and they seem worthless!" I complained to my friends. "Doesn't my experience count for anything?" I whined to my sister's cat that I envied for not having to get a job, much less its own food.

But eventually I did secure a job, albeit at Radio Shack near the high school I graduated from. I felt so humiliated that I hid in the office when anyone I knew walked in. But my car note didn't care where I worked, so I had to sell those batteries and cell phones. However, I kept sending out resumes while working at "the shack," as one of my girlfriends teasingly called it. Two months later I was offered a job more in my field that I kept until I left for New York to work on my master's degree. What's odd, however, is that I almost didn't want to take the new job because I had finally gotten over my stuck-up self and had become a pretty good saleswoman.

As you are searching for a job, keep in mind that the job search process can be a long and tedious one for both the recent graduate and the seasoned, yet unemployed professional. It may take you months to land the type of job you're searching for. Until you find a job relevant to your career, consider your job search as your temporary full-time job—one that doesn't pay anything but has good benefits.

The job search tactics you use can mean the difference between a slightly mind-numbing job search experience and a painful one. Instead of playing hit or miss, you should take calculated steps to secure a job and jumpstart your career. Once you've decided on the career you want, your goal should be to seek out those companies or organizations that offer jobs relative to your career aspirations. Make a point of thinking outside the box when starting your job search. Newspapers, magazines, and television stations aren't the only entities looking for people with communication degrees who want to work as writers and editors. There are others places hiring teachers besides public and private schools. And hospitals aren't the only place where nurses work. The faster you are able to recognize not so blatant opportunities, the closer you will be to getting hired for a job you'll enjoy.

JOB SEARCH STRATEGIES

While many people rely on the more formal methods of job searching, such as through newspapers and employment agencies, the best way to secure a job is by using both formal and informal strategies. Informal strategies, such as job searching through networking and contacting employers directly, will take more time on your behalf, but are worth the effort. Studies have shown that approximately two-thirds of jobs are found and secured by using informal search strategies, while only around one-third of jobs are obtained through formal methods.

Formal Job Search Strategies

Newspaper Ads: Millions of people look in papers across the U.S. for job listings every week, but only as few as five percent of jobs are ever advertised in a newspaper. And when you do find a job advertised in the newspaper, you'll probably have to compete with the hundreds of other people who saw the ad and are applying for the job too. Bottom line: Don't rely solely on newspapers to find a job. When you do find a listing that interests you, apply for the position immediately. Also keep in mind that most newspapers have websites now. Their website will allow you to check for job listings everyday so you don't have to constantly buy papers.

Employment/Staffing Agencies: Many employment agencies get paid by companies to find employees, so they can be extremely helpful in finding you a position that interests you, or to at least get you working somewhere while you're still job searching. Some employment agencies are very industry-specific, only dealing with techies or business professionals, for example. Look for an agency that specializes in placing people within your field before you go with one that works on a broader scale.

Internet Ads: There are tons of sites on the Internet with job listings, but you'll have to search out the ones that are worth browsing. You can search sites like Monster.com that have listings for nearly every field in every city, city-specific sites like those for city government jobs, and field-specific sites like ones for counselors. Of course, the more sites you visit the more jobs you'll see. Some websites and job listings are not kept up to date, however. If you find a great listing that doesn't show the date it was posted, call the company to see if they are still hiring for the position and if they have any other positions open that fit your interests.

Job Fairs: Job fairs offer a convenient way for you to market yourself and learn more about companies hiring for positions you might be interested in. Always dress like you are going to an interview, and bring plenty of resumes and business cards.

Informal Job Search Strategies

Direct Mail Campaigns: This is a "wait and see" strategy. After identifying companies that offer (but may not be hiring for) positions in your field, you mail the hiring manager a customized cover letter and resume and hope you get a response. You'll need to be quick about following up on all the mail you send out to make the most of this approach.

Alumni Associations: Check with your alma mater to see if they offer placement services for their graduates. If the alumni association provides a list of alumni and the fields they now work in, take the initiative to call those working in your field for job leads.

Your Personal Network: Tell all your friends and relatives about the type of jobs you are searching for so they can also be on the lookout for you. If you have certain relatives or friends that have a knack for networking, give them a couple of copies of your resume—you never know who they'll meet.

Cold Calling: If you learn of a company that seems interesting, but don't know if they are hiring, there's nothing wrong with calling the hiring manager to find out. Just make sure you talk to the manager. Never listen to anyone who doesn't have the ability to hire you when they tell you there are no current job openings. When you speak to managers tell them about your interests and the career you want to pursue. Perhaps if they are not hiring they can tell you about similar companies that are.

Unannounced Visits: You're harder for managers to brush off if you're in their face trying to get a job. The downside is you could also be annoying. Before making an unannounced visit, do a little investigating to find out when the person you'll need to see will be in. Dress like you're expecting an interview and bring more than one resume. If the person you need to speak to is busy, ask if you can wait. If it seems as if you might be waiting for too long then leave a copy of your resume and follow up with the person via phone the next day.

Professional Organizations: Joining an organization relative to your career is a great way to network with people who can give you leads on job openings within your field. Many organizations provide members with lists on who's hiring or have companies constantly recruiting people specifically from their organization. Find and join a professional organization in your city as soon as possible.

Volunteerism: Volunteering is an excellent way to network with people working in different fields. The people you meet may open you up to job opportunities you never considered.

NO-NO'S WHILE JOB HUNTING

Having an unprofessional email address: How seriously do you think you'll be taken by an employer if you email your resume from sweetlikecandy69@hotmail.com? Not very seriously at all. If you haven't done so, take a few minutes to sign up for a free email account and put your name or part of your name as the email address.

Having an unprofessional voice message: Talking sexy on your answering machine or having vulgar music playing in the background will turn a potential employer all the way off. While you're job searching you'll need to leave a very professional message on your phone line so an employer won't get the wrong impression of you.

Chapter 3

Applying for Positions

"Few great men would have got past personnel."
—Paul Goodman

Sometimes it seems the most you can do is wish your resume well after you send it off. But there is something else you can do: make sure it ends up in the hands of the right person. The *right* hands are the ones that belong to the person who can say "you're hired."

Sending your materials to the right person is easy when the job advertisement directs you to send it to a specific person, but trickier when you are asked to send it to human resources. Most large organizations and companies now have human resources (HR) departments, which serve as the middle-man between potential employees and the employers. The people who work in HR are the ones who decide if your resume merits the consideration of the person hiring for the position. You take the gamble of your resume ever getting seriously looked at when you send it to these well-meaning, but career-blocking people. To overcome this barrier you can find out who your resume really needs to go to and send it to them and the human resources department. Finding out who the real decision maker is may take a little time and snooping, but it's worth it. The most direct approach is by just calling the company and asking who's who. If that doesn't suit you then browse their website. Finding the right person shouldn't be that hard. For example, if you are applying for an accounting position within a university, it makes the most sense to send your resume to someone whose title is accounting manager. If you are applying for an advertising job within a newspaper company, you would most likely end up being hired by the advertising director.

Once you know who your materials should be directed to you're one step closer to getting your valuables into their hands. Keep in mind that just because you sent your resume off doesn't mean that it was received and reviewed. Some employers get hundreds of applications every week and you don't want yours to be the one that gets lost on the way to their desk. The following are simple rules to follow when sending your application materials via mail, fax, email, or when delivering them in person.

By mail: When applying by mail, print your resume and cover letter on matching resume paper. If your line of work requires samples that can be sent (such as photographs, graphics, or news stories), send the samples that reflect your best work and put your full name and contact information on them. Send your materials in an envelope that matches your resume and cover letter, or in a paper-sized envelope so your materials will be neat when received. Call the employer two to three days after they should have received your materials to make sure they got them, to inquire if they have any questions for you, and to ask any questions you may have about the company (unless you are specifically directed not to contact the employer).

By Fax: When sending your resume and cover letter via fax, make doubly sure the cover sheet is directed to the right person. Wait a few minutes after you send it to call and verify that it was received, and that your materials are in the process of being given to the person who should review it. It won't hurt to call later in the day to make sure it got into the right person's hands, to inquire if they have any questions for you, and to ask any questions you may have about the company.

By Email: If you're directed to email your resume to a specific person, call the person to verify that it was received a few hours after you sent it, to inquire if they have any questions for you, and to ask any questions you may have about the company.
If you are applying online or have no idea who will receive your resume, call the HR office and ask someone to check to make sure all your materials were received.

In Person: Applying in person gives you the chance to present yourself to a potential employer and to take a look at your potential workplace. Call the company and ask when the owner or manager will be in on the day you plan to visit. It is a good idea to dress business casual or in an actual suit. Ask for the person in charge once you get there, and if they are not there ask for the next person in charge. Your goal is to introduce yourself to someone who has some decision-making authority when it comes to getting you a job with the company. If you have to turn your materials in to someone in human resources, inquire about their hiring process and how long it usually takes for materials to be reviewed. Always be extra nice to everyone you meet while visiting the company.

Chapter 4

Preparing for the Interview

"Success depends upon previous preparation, and without such preparation there is sure to be failure."
—Confucius

Getting that long-awaited phone call for an interview can be a big confidence booster. It means the cover letter and resume you hoped would impress your potential employer did, and your phone calls, emails or drop-by visits weren't in vain. So be optimistic. You're now closer to getting a call saying you're hired. But just how do you make that happen? You prepare for the interview 10 times more than you would prepare for a date with the man of your dreams. How well you're prepared for the interview will dictate how well you'll do once it's begun.

The following fours tasks should be handled before you walk in to greet any employer.

TASK 1: RESEARCH THE COMPANY

Before you step into an interview you should have researched the company as much as possible to help you better answer and ask questions. You can gather information from many sources, including the company's website, their marketing materials, and employees you may know. Here are some things you can find out:

- The company's mission.
- How long the company has been in business and who started it.
- The company's products and/or services.
- How successful the company is compared to others within the industry.
- How well the company is doing financially.
- How many employees the company has.
- If the company has offices in other cities, states or countries.
- The company's recruitment process.
- The company's future plans.

If you take time to gather this information you'll be a step ahead of other applicants who didn't see the need to do their research. You'll be better able to talk about what you like about the company and discuss aspects of the company that the interviewer may bring up.

TASK 2: PRACTICE INTERVIEWING

Perhaps one of the most unnerving parts of the interview process is when the employer takes out his trusty sheet full of interview questions and smiles. Right then you know it's time for you to either sink or swim. In order for you to swim you need to understand the purpose of the question-and-answer phase of the interview. The questions posed by employers, no matter how mundane or unusual, simply give them a chance to gauge the following:

- Your personality.
- If you can help meet the company's wants, needs, and goals.

- Your wants, needs, and goals.
- If you will fit into the company's culture.

Just as your cover letter should be tailored to an employer, so should the answers to the questions posed. The more you've researched the company and its needs, the better you'll be able to answer the questions to an employer's liking.

For example, if you know the job requires you to work a lot in teams, then of course you "enjoy collaborating with other co-workers to complete assignments." The employer doesn't need to know you really prefer working alone! If the position requires you to learn new software programs, then you certainly "are sure learning new programs will not pose a problem for you." The employer doesn't need to know you'll have to re-read the software manual a dozen times at home! Employers know that people are rarely perfectly suited for a position. However, you don't want an employer to eliminate you as a candidate because of small weaknesses you blabbed you have. Now, if the employer asks you if you speak Spanish and you say yes when you don't know what "agua" means, then you'll be in trouble.

Answering the interview questions can be like walking on a tight rope. You want to appear confident but not cocky, knowledgeable but not a know-it-all, energetic but not wired, and poised but not "posed" for the interview. And just as important, you don't want to say anything incorrect or silly. This is why practicing for each interview is so important.

The following are sample interview questions and possible ways to answer them. Have an older professional ask you the questions during a mock interview.

Sample Interview Questions:

1. Can you tell me a little about yourself?
First briefly go over your academic background, work history and what led you to the career you're entering. Then you can talk about anything interesting/unusual about yourself

that is positive, like you've traveled to several countries, are a trained dancer or ice skater, or volunteer in community service programs. Do not give the interviewer your whole life story, say anything negative about yourself, discuss your political or religious views, or divulge private details of your life.

2. *Why are you seeking a position with this company?*
Discuss certain aspects of the company that you admire, such as its reputation or mission, and how working for the company will help you reach your career goals.

3. *What makes you qualified to apply for this position?*
Discuss how your educational background, work history, and the skills you've acquired have prepared you for the exact position you are applying for.

4. *Why do you want this position?*
Explain why the position is a perfect fit for you, given your educational background, work history or interests. Talk about specific aspects of the job that you'll enjoy and what you like about the company.

5. *Why should I hire you?*
Again, discuss how your educational background, work history, and the skills you've acquired have prepared you for the exact position you are applying for. However, also highlight your positive character traits, like your creativity or perceptiveness, and how having someone in the position with these traits will benefit the company. You should also talk about anything else that you think may set you apart from other candidates.

6. *If hired, how long will you stay with the company?*
Stress to the employer that you can really see yourself growing with the company, and that you see the company

as a great place to start and build your career. Employers know you don't know the answer to this question; they just want to make sure you aren't using the position as an "in-between" job until you find something better.

7. *What are your career ambitions?*
Discuss your ultimate career objectives and how the position you are applying for, and the company itself, will help you meet those objectives. Do not discuss career goals that have nothing to do with the field you're in (i.e. you are applying for a financial counselor position, but you say your career goal is to become a wedding planner.)

8. *Why did you choose this career field?*
Discuss what first drew you to the field you're in, and what aspects about the field made you passionate enough to want to build a career in it.

9. *What is your ideal type of company?*
The ideal type of company you describe should closely resemble the company you're trying to join. After describing this "imaginary" place you can talk about what you like most about the company you're hoping to be a part of.

10. *What kind of people do you enjoy/dislike working with?*
First, stress that you are able and enjoy working with all types of people. Next, describe the type of people you enjoy working with most (like flexible or humorous people). Then pick a type of person that no-one wants to work with (such as someone who badmouths other co-workers).

11. *What things are most important to you on a job?*
Discuss what you need most in a position to enjoy it (as long as the position offers these benefits), such as the ability to interact with lots of people, room to grow, or supportive co-workers and managers.

12. Do you prefer working alone or with a team?
Stress that you are able to work well in a team or alone and talk about what you like about both. Then consider the position. If it requires you to work most often in teams then that's what you prefer, and vice versa.

13. What qualities do you look for in a manager?
Discuss the positive attributes that you most admire in people and why you look for these attributes in a manager (such as someone who is easy to talk to). If you have worked for a manager that you really liked you can briefly talk about him or her.

14. What is your greatest strength/weakness?
Tell the employer you don't like trick questions. Just kidding. Discuss your strengths first, such as your strong work ethic, ability to explain hard to understand things in a simple way, or your patience. For your weakness, pick an attribute that is good to have sometimes, but can still be considered a character flaw, like being impatient with certain types of people, or being a perfectionist when it comes to projects you're responsible for.

15. Do you have any additional skills that make you a good candidate for the position?
Discuss any talents or skills you may have that aren't a requirement for the position, and explain how they can add to your effectiveness on the job.

16. What did you like most/least about your former boss?
Discuss the qualities you liked most in your boss first and what you learned from him or her. If you had a particularly good working relationship with your former boss, then you can talk briefly about how well you worked together. When asked what you liked least about him or her, pick something relatively minor, like your boss' forgetfulness. Do

not badmouth your former boss or co-workers.

17. *In what ways did you contribute to your last company?*
Discuss specific ways you helped the company, such as increasing profits, implementing a new service, or finding a great solution to a problem that was hurting the company. You can also talk about how you performed well in your position day-to-day, and how doing your job well positively impacted your co-workers, managers, and the company as a whole.

18. *What problems did you encounter at your former company and how did you deal with them?*
Discuss problems you had that didn't involve confrontations with your boss or co-workers, such as having an inflexible schedule or not being given enough direction on hard assignments. Then explain how you dealt professionally and maturely with whatever problem you mentioned.

19. *How would your co-workers describe you?*
Pick your best qualities that your co-workers generally liked, like your good sense of humor or friendliness. If possible, pick qualities that would have made you well-respected, such as being a hard worker or straightforward and honest.

20. *Are you comfortable working with a diverse group of people?*
The answer is always yes. Talk about why you enjoy working with people from different backgrounds (you're exposed to different cultures or beliefs, which can help you grow as a person). You can then briefly share any positive experience you have had that allowed you to work with a diverse group of people.

After the practice interview session ask the person helping you the following questions:

- How confident you came across.
- Your demeanor while answering questions.
- If you answered the questions intelligently and concisely.
- If you answered all of the questions fully.
- Which questions you seemed to have difficulty with.
- What you might need to improve upon.

TASK 3: BRAINSTORM QUESTIONS FOR THE EMPLOYER

Asking questions about the company and your position further communicates your interest. All questions you feel are appropriate and relevant are game, except questions about money. Employers generally feel it is inappropriate and too soon to talk about how much your salary will be until you're offered the position. You can memorize the questions you have prepared or bring a copy of the questions. Here are a few examples:

1. What qualities do you look for in an employee?
2. What is the company's culture like?
3. What is your management philosophy?
4. What will be expected of me as a new employee?
5. What level of supervision will be given to me?
6. Does the company make a point of promoting from within?
7. How does the employee review and evaluation process work?
8. What is a typical day like for an employee with my job title?
9. Is the owner/manager easily accessible to employees?
10. What type of benefits does the company offer?

TASK 4: GET YOUR WARDROBE TOGETHER

Take the idea of dressing to impress very seriously because it isn't just your credentials that will be judged during the interview. Your appearance should be as sharp as you are. Your attire, hair, make-up and accessories must reflect a professional woman that means business. Now, the problem is that different people have different ideas about what is appropriate business attire. Some women will walk into an interview looking like they should be going to a club and think their outfit is cute. Others will stroll in dressed business casual because they don't feel like the job they're applying for warrants wearing a nice suit. However, during the interview only one person's opinion about fashion counts—the interviewer's opinion. And because you can never be sure about just what someone else thinks is tasteful, you're better off playing it safe by sticking to what has traditionally been considered "proper" attire for an interview.

This can sometimes be a problem for women with a flair for fashion and accessories. Keep in mind that you'll have plenty of time to show off your fashion sense after you've gotten the job. While you're trying to get one you'll have to play by a conservative set of rules for attire.

Rules for Attire

Do . . .

✓ Wear a suit to the interview, choosing between one with a skirt, dress or pants.

✓ Stick with solid colored or pinstriped suits. Most people opt for a navy blue, black or brown suit.

✓ Choose a suit made from a natural synthetic blend material, cotton-polyester, or wool. The suit should be tailored to fit you.

✓ If you opt for a skirt or dress pay close attention to how short it is on you. You don't want to be ashamed to cross your legs during the interview.

✓ Wear a blouse that matches well with your suit, opting for a long sleeved one that will allow the cuff to show around a quarter or half-inch beyond the jacket sleeve.

✓ Wear shoes with a closed toe, even if it's summer time. The heel should be no more than 1 1/2 inches high. The shoes should compliment your suit.

✓ Wear hose closest to your skin tone or black if you're wearing a black suit.

Definitely Do Not . . .

✗ Try to get away with wearing a business casual outfit. You're dressing for the interview, not the job.

✗ Wear a loud colored suit or one with designs or animal prints.

✗ Choose a suit made from materials that wrinkle easily, or that looks cheap just from the look of it.

✗ Come into the interview wearing a skirt, pants or dress that is too tight or too big for you. You should feel and look comfortable in your clothes.

✗ Wear no blouse or undershirt at all.

✗ Wear heels you can't walk in or ones that look worn out.

✗ Wear hose with fancy designs or with a little run in them. In fact, you should bring an extra pair with you when wearing a dress or skirt.

Those rules for attire aren't too hard to follow, and neither are these other rules governing fragrance, jewelry, make-up, accessories and hairstyles.

Fragrance: Pay special attention to how you smell. Sniff yourself if you're unsure! If the perfume you wear is strong with just one spray, then opt for a nice smelling body spray for the day. Make sure you don't smell like any kind of food (a burger you ate before the interview) or animal (a cat you may have at home) or cigarettes and alcohol.

Jewelry: Less is better. Don't try to "bling bling" for the interview. Lose any tongue, nose, chin or eyebrow rings unless you're interviewing for positions where you'll look out of place without them (which isn't many places).

Make-up: Again, less is better. You want to look natural, not *made up*. Save the heavy blush, fake eye lashes and seductive eye shadow for another day.

Accessories: A small purse that matches your suit is fine for the interview, but it's better to just bring a small briefcase that holds extra copies of your resume and work samples. A scarf around your neck that matches the suit is okay, but it should have a simple design.

Hairstyles: Black women are recognized around the globe for their creativity when it comes to hairstyles. We can sport a flip on Monday, an elegant upswept hairdo on Tuesday, and show off a beautiful braided style on Wednesday. Most of us hopefully appreciate our hair's versatility. However, some decision makers in corporate America and even those who run smaller businesses just can't understand what it is we do with our hair. Some employers—even black ones—deem hairstyles like braids, twists, and locks as inappropriate for the workplace and too "ethnic." So sadly, the way you wear your hair to the interview may unfortunately work against you when interviewing with very conservative-minded individuals. This is an ignorant and bigoted truth, but it's the truth nonetheless. So what do you do? Many women and men refuse to compromise their hairstyles to fit someone else's image of what's appropriate. I, for example, have worn my hair in twists or braids to every interview since college. I believe that if a company rules me out because of my hairstyle, I probably won't feel comfortable working there anyway. Others view changing their hairstyles for the interview or work as just "playing the game." How you wear your hair to the interview is entirely up to you. However, there are some rules for hairstyles that should be common sense. These include coming in with neat hair no matter what the style, leaving out unnecessary hair accessories, and making sure you have absolutely no dandruff to be embarrassed about.

Chapter 5

Twenty Pointers to a Better Interview

"When you're prepared, you're more confident. When you have a strategy, you're more comfortable."
—Fred Couples

You only get one chance to convince an employer to hire you. Avoid playing the woulda, coulda, shoulda game by following these 20 interviewing rules on all of your interviews.

1. Arrive Ahead of Time: Get good directions and plan to arrive at the place you're being interviewed at least 20 minutes early so you won't be 20 minutes late. You never know if there will be a lot of traffic or how hard it will be to find a parking space.

2. Give Your Appearance a Double Check: Take time to straighten yourself up before greeting the interviewer. Check your clothes, hair, make-up, breath and odor.

3. Be Cordial to Everyone You Meet at the Company: The person interviewing you might end up being the same person you let the elevator door shut on during the way up to the interview. Briefly greet and be nice to everyone at the company because you never know just who has a say in your hiring.

4. Make a Good First Impression: Consider it showtime when employers first spot you. From that very moment they are sizing you up. Try to feel their vibe so you can make them feel at ease with you before the interview begins.

5. Be Respectful of the Employer: Don't forget whom you're talking to. Greet the people interviewing you with their last name until they tell you otherwise. Leave the slang at home and turn the cell phone or pager off—not on vibrate.

6. Watch Your Body Language: Your demeanor should exude confidence and enthusiasm, which can be shown in various ways, including a firm handshake, eye-to-eye contact, good posture, and a sincere smile. Definite don'ts include biting your lip or nails, slouching in your chair, excessive note-taking, watching the clock, fiddling your hands or feet, and looking at everything else in the room but the interviewer while talking.

7. Have Extra Copies of Your Resume: You may be required to interview with more than one person. Being able to hand them a crisp resume demonstrates your professionalism and thoughtfulness.

8. Listen Thoughtfully to All Questions and Think Before You Speak: Always make sure you understand a question before you go about answering it. People can tell when you're running off at the mouth while trying to remember what you were asked. Ask for clarification if you don't completely understand a question.

9. Answer Questions Completely: Try not to give simple yes or no answers. One of your goals is to show how well you communicate with others.

10. Stress the Skills You Can Offer the Company: Know the exact skills an employer is looking for and stress that you have these skills and enjoy using them. Also talk about any other skills you have that are not required for your position, but that you feel will make you more attractive to an employer, such as bilingualism or public speaking.

11. Stress Your Ability To Learn New Skills Fast: If there's a skill you lack that an employer asks about, stress your ability to quickly learn that skill, possibly giving examples of how you've learned fast in other situations.

12. Stress Your Positive Personality: Communicate with the interviewer how easy you are to work with, how you can see the silver lining in any cloud, and how you're so very flexible, ect. The employer is looking for someone who current employees will get along with.

13. Talk With Pride About Your Accomplishments: Most employers believe that past performance is the best indicator of future performance. Make them realize how valuable you are by talking about accomplishments you're proud of.

14. Be Prepared for Tough Questions: While most interview questions are to be expected, some interviewers may surprise you with a curve ball. An employer knows when they've asked a hard question and probably just wants to see how you'll react. Impress them. When asked a question that makes you say "hmmmm," stay calm, take time to think of a good response, and try your best to answer the question as if it didn't faze you.

15. Tell Them Why You Want The Job: Don't let the interview come to an end without telling the person interviewing you why you want the job and what it is that you like so much about the position. This further demonstrates your enthusiasm and that you aren't just applying for the paycheck.

16. Have Any Work Samples Ready To Show: Be ready to whip out work samples you've brought for the employer to review. You shouldn't have to search for anything, and if you do it makes you look unprepared. Don't let the interview end without showing the employer your work samples, even if he or she didn't ask to see them.

17. Give Examples of How You've Handled Tough or Sticky Situations: Show the employer that you can handle any job and how resourceful you are by relating stories of how you've handled sticky situations very well.

18. Don't Undermine Yourself: Never talk negatively about yourself or talk about what you can't or won't do, no matter how insignificant you think what you're saying is.

19. Don't Badmouth Anyone: Never badmouth a past employer or your former co-workers—regardless of how comfortable you feel while talking to someone interviewing you.

20. Leave a Great Lasting Impression: No matter how good or bad you think the interview went, the show isn't over until you're out of the employer's sight. Be as cordial and enthusiastic at the end of the interview as you were at the beginning. Communicate with the employer that you are genuinely interested in the position and that you'd very much like to work for the company. Make sure you shake the hand of everyone you've interviewed with. Take time to tell them how much you appreciate being interviewed, to find out when you should hear from them, and to wish them a great day.

The most interesting interview experience I have had was with a national newsletter publishing company. The company needed a temporary research editor while one of its employees was on maternity leave. After interviewing and taking a very hard test for an employment agency, I had to go through three more interviews with those inside the publishing company. The interviews were set back-to-back.

The first interview was with the managing editor. She instantly came across as friendly but strictly about business. She asked me a succession of questions about my qualifications and work history, but also made me feel comfortable by talking about what she liked about the company and what I might like about the position. She then asked me to do a typesetting exercise on a computer. I thought the interview went well and she told me I did great on the exercise.

The next interview was with a senior research editor who I would be working closely with. I thought the purpose of this interview was to see if I would fit in her group. The lady who interviewed me was very sweet and seemed sincerely interested in who I was as a person. She wanted to know what I was passionate about, what my ultimate career goal was, and how I would use the job to get there. I talked to her for what seemed like a long time, and walked away from that interview feeling that it went extremely well.

By the time I got to the third interview, which was with the human resources manager, I felt very confident. That confidence lasted about two seconds. The person I was introduced to, a black woman and one of a handful of minorities at the company, scared me for some reason. To this day I still don't know what it was. She was dressed really regally in a long, flowing dress and had this piercing gaze. I felt like if I said or did anything wrong she would call my mother and tell her she raised me wrong. She turned out to be very down-to-earth, however, and we ended up talking quite frankly about her expectations of me, what I could offer the company, and my background.

My confidence was almost back up to sea level until she asked me what my favorite word was. "My favorite word?" I asked her, thinking I had heard her wrong. She nodded yes, and said as an editor I should have a favorite word.

The question should have been an easy one, as I have words that I like for one reason or another. However, as soon as I began to think of one all the words I had ever known seemed to fly out of my brain. "I'll have to give that question some more thought," I said meekly after three minutes had passed. She looked supremely disappointed, but shook my hand, wished me well and sent me home. I left feeling like a complete loser.

On the train ride home, one of my favorite words finally came to me—fierce. I emailed her the word when I got home with a note about how sorry I was that it took me so long to think of it. I guess she liked the word and everyone else who interviewed me thought I was a good fit because I was offered the job two days later.

Following Up After the Interview

Sending a thank-you note to your interviewer is a good practice. It shows courtesy, respect, and that you really do want the job. Send it through the mail the same or next day after your interview. You can write a note on a blank card or send a typed letter on resume paper in a matching envelope. Thank the employer for the opportunity to interview for the position, and reiterate your interest in working for the company.

If the people who interviewed you have not contacted you when they said they would then give them a call. Let them know that you're calling to check on the status of their hiring process and that you're still very interested in the position.

Chapter 6

Learning From Rejection

". . . Count it all joy when you fall into various trials, knowing that the testing of your faith produces patience. But let patience have its perfect work, that you may be perfect and complete, lacking nothing."
—James 1- 2:4, New King James Bible

"You didn't get the job?" Don't you hate it when people ask that question right after you told them you didn't get it!? It's okay to pout a little, but it's not okay to get depressed and let your discouragement keep you from being optimistic about the next interview.

I actually cried the first time I didn't get a position I thought I was destined to have. After the second time I sulked around the house. Did I come off as too confident? I wondered. Did I not smile enough? Did I not get hired because I was black? I asked myself a dozen pointless questions like those in between checking my dwindling savings account. Well, the questions themselves weren't pointless, but my dwelling on them and bringing myself down in the process was. I stopped muttering how life "just isn't fair" after my mother kindly let me know that I wasn't the only person praying for a job.

Understand that when you're competing with people for a position someone isn't going to get it. Unfortunately, sometimes that someone may be you. But you shouldn't view a rejection letter or phone call as an insult or barrier to your achievement. You don't know what God has in store for you. Focus on how you can do better next time. You may have not been chosen for any number of reasons. It might just be that you were great, but someone was better qualified than you. You can't help that. The following are various reasons employers give for not offering someone a position:

1. Poor personal appearance
2. Overly aggressive
3. Inability to express information clearly
4. Lack of interest and enthusiasm
5. Lack of planning for career; no purpose and goals
6. Nervousness, lack of confidence and poise
7. Overemphasis on money
8. Unwilling to start at the bottom
9. Lack of tact and courtesy
10. Lack of maturity
11. Negative attitude about past employers
12. No genuine interest in company or job
13. No eye contact with the interviewer
14. Application form is incomplete or sloppy
15. No sense of humor
16. Late for interview
17. Failure to express appreciation for interviewer's time
18. Failure to ask questions about the job
19. Gives vague responses to questions

From Reason's People Don't Get Hired, published in Creative Job Search by the Minnesota Department of Economic Security, copyright holder; used with permission.

If you really want to know why you didn't get the position, simply ask the person who interviewed you. Be very tactful and explain that you're inquiring so that you can be more successful on your next interview.

After taking a day to debate whether or not I should ask a woman who had interviewed me why I didn't get the job, I finally picked up the phone and called her. I had applied for an entry-level position as an editorial assistant for the children's books division at a publishing house. I was qualified for the position, had what I considered one of my best interview experiences, and the woman who interviewed me actually told me how impressed she was with me before I left the interview. So naturally, I was dumbfounded and upset.

The lady told me the only reason why she didn't choose me was because she thought I really wouldn't like the job. She said while I was interested in working on books, I had more of an interest in working on non-fiction or adult fiction, not children's literature, and she thought that people should work on what they really love. She then said she would notify me when an opening came up in a different division, and would personally recommend me, which she eventually did.

After I got off the phone I realized she was right. I wanted to work at the company (which is why I had applied), but I was not sincerely interested in working on children's books. In fact, when I initially applied for the position, I immediately thought about how if I got that job I could probably transfer to a different department in half a year.

Someone who loved children's books deserved that job, and I hope the person who she hired loved the position.

The job you need and deserve is closer than you think. Wait for it.

Chapter 7

Finding & Keeping a Career Mentor

*"No matter what great things you
accomplish, somebody helps you."*
—*Wilma Rudolph*

I've been blessed with wonderful people over the years that have served as my mentors. These people, who have included grade school teachers, college professors, employers, and individuals working in my industry, have helped me make important decisions that led me to where I am now in my life. Mentors can help you with any number of issues, and you can have various people who serve as mentors advise you on different aspects of your life, including your career.

Finding a career mentor should be number two on your "to do" list—right after what's probably getting a job. A career mentor, someone who is dedicated to helping you succeed in your career, is an invaluable person to have in your life. A career mentor can help you with the following:

- Make decisions regarding your choice of jobs.
- Avoid pitfalls in your job search.
- Find vacant positions in your field.
- Give you information about your field.
- Help you meet people to further your career.
- Give you a realistic view of what working in your field is really like.
- Give you pointers on how to succeed in your field.
- Give you salary information.
- Inform you on appropriate business etiquette.
- Advise you on how to handle problems in your workplace.

Like friendships, career mentor relationships are formed over time. In most cases, mentors are acquired through befriending people you meet that are in a position to help you.

If you haven't met anyone you consider "mentor material" then you should seek someone out. Search for someone successful in your field at organizational meetings, conferences, career fairs and other venues. You can even find potential mentors in magazines and newsletters. I found my first New York-based career mentor in the pages of *Black Issues Book Review*. She was being profiled in the magazine after having left a wonderful position as a senior editor at a major publishing house to start her own literary agency. I contacted her immediately through email, and though it took about a month or so of polite nudging in the form of more emails and a phone call or two, she eventually agreed to meet with me, and in fact invited me out to lunch. We clicked right away and I was glad I was so persistent. That one email eventually led to an internship and my being able to learn from someone with years of experience in the field I was interested in.

When you chance upon a potential mentor introduce yourself as a young professional seeking information from successful and knowledgeable sources like them. Potential mentors can be male or female and any ethnicity. The only thing they must eventually have is a desire to help you.

Once you've found a mentor make sure to nurture the relationship by showing your appreciation for the advice and whatever else your mentor provides. You don't want them to get the feeling they're being taken advantage of. You can show your appreciation by sincere "thank you's" as well as cards, flowers or lunch. Remember that because career mentor relationships are like friendships, you have to keep in contact with your mentors. Don't just call on them when you need something. Consider them and treat them as you would a good friend. Do this, and you'll have someone in your corner for life.

Sample Letter to Potential Career Mentor

Dear Ms. Jessica Lowe,

I hope this letter finds you in good spirits and health. My name is Divona Phillips. I am writing you because I saw an article written on your career and recent promotion to Editorial Director at Berington Press in January's issue of *Publisher's Weekly*. I also remember reading about you in *Essence* some time ago. While I have come across many African-American journalists in NYC, I have yet to meet someone working in the field of book publishing. I know there is much I could learn from you.

I recently moved to New York City from Colorado where I had worked as an editorial assistant for a weekly newspaper after graduating from college in May of 2005. I relocated here because I finally realized I had a passion for books, not newspapers, and Colorado was not the place where I could pursue my ambitions. I hope to work my way up in the book publishing industry (as an editor) and eventually own a small press dedicated to publishing African-American literature and self-help books. At 23, I am currently pursuing my master's in English, and working as an intern for a small children's book publisher.

I would love an opportunity to talk with you about your experiences in the book publishing industry, and would be so very grateful for any advice you could give me in relation to my goals. Perhaps I could take you to lunch? I can be reached via phone at 212-212-1212 or by email at dphillips@aol.com.

Sincerely,
Divona Phillips
Divona Phillips

Chapter 8

Staying Positive

"If thou faint in the day of adversity, thy strength is small."
—Proverbs 24:10, New King James Bible

All of us are traveling on different roads, going to different destinations. Sometimes we can guess where we may end up, and perhaps even navigate our road so well that we get to the place we hoped for ahead of time. But the only thing we can truly be sure about as we travel is that our road is not a straight one. We have to expect twists and turns. Slippery slopes, hills that become mountains, and roads with no end in sight should not take us by surprise or frighten us into turning around. They should motivate us to go forward, at a faster pace, and with greater determination.

There are many personal qualities we will need to have on our journey. Some we may have when we first start walking on our road; others may be instilled in us along the way. Patience, determination, faith, hope, diligence and industriousness are just a few of the qualities needed on our journey. There is one quality, however, that must be stressed above the others. If you lack this quality you may not even find a road to travel on. This quality is a positive attitude.

You can't secure the future you're planning without a positive attitude. One of your greatest strengths must be your ability to see the beauty in your personal thunderstorms, and not let your frustrations dampen your passion. Your hopes, your dreams, your smallest goals cannot be realized if you lack a positive attitude.

Your positive attitude will help you build the career you thought you didn't have the tools to build. Your positive attitude will bring you out of the worst of circumstances. Your positive attitude will allow you to do better than the people who had it easier and better than you starting out in their careers. It's your positive attitude that will allow you to look back on your life in your old age and wonder how you accomplished so much.

You have but one choice to make: whether you are going to pursue your dreams or not. And if you decide your dreams are worth toiling for then you're one step closer to making each of them a reality. Just remember to always keep your positive attitude with you on your journey.

Part 2
Succeeding in the Real World

Chapter 9

Letting Go of Real World Myths

"If you have a job without any aggravations, you don't have a job."
—Malcolm S. Forbes

All college graduates end up asking the question. It's just a matter of when. It may be our fifth month on the job, or perhaps our fifth year, but sooner or later we begin to wonder why someone didn't tell us that life after college isn't all it's cracked up to be.

I started asking this about one year after I graduated. I wanted to get my college tuition back after finding out that 1) having two degrees mattered just as much as having two high school diplomas when no one was hiring; 2) if I wanted any chance of making $45,000 a year in an entry-level position, I had better go back to school and major in computer science; 3) a "great" job can turn into a "bad" job faster than celebrities divorce; and 4) people on *The Real World* actually had it much easier than I did.

Well, the reason we weren't told that life after college isn't exactly easy is simple: If we knew how frustrating working for a living could sometimes be, we might not have focused on graduating. And our professors and parents couldn't have that! So perhaps that's why some of them gave us the impression that life after college would be easier than college life.

We were told many things about how life after college would be, and some of us may have gotten a tad bit misinformed. In fact, in college we may have heard of, and began to believe, many myths about the real world. Some of these myths can hurt us in the long run if we cling to them because they keep us from looking at the real world realistically, and carrying ourselves accordingly. The following are five myths that belong in a fairytale.

Myth #1: Your Degree Guarantees You a Great Job: Throughout high school and college many of us were told that our degree would guarantee us a great job and career. Yet at the same time we were told that nothing in life is guaranteed. It's true that your degree will get you into interviews a high school diploma can't, and will make you more likely to land a great job and build an impressive career. But a college degree shouldn't be mistaken for a magic wand. There are plenty of college graduates who go for months and sometimes years waiting for that superb job and career. They'll be the first ones to tell you that a degree can be overrated. And if a degree is the only thing you've got going for you then you'd better have a dozen of them. It's your hard work and ambition combined with your degree that will unlock doors for you.

Myth #2: Your Degree Guarantees You a Great Salary: Throughout high school and college many of us were also shown charts highlighting how much more a college graduate can make over a lifetime than someone with just a high school diploma, excluding Bill Gates. We were led to assume that a degree equated to lots and lots of money. So it's not surprising that some college graduates think they're on *Punked* when they're offered a job that pays a little over $10 an hour. They start to feel like they wasted their time getting a degree, and that's not it at all. They should have been told that their salary would depend on the type of degree they earned, the career they chose, the company they worked for, the city they lived in, their experience, and a dozen other factors.

Myth #3: Do What You Love and You'll Never Have To Work: This is a catchy little phrase, but unfortunately it's just not true. If you do what you love you'll feel that your life has more meaning, your whole focus won't be on how much your job pays, and you'll undoubtedly be much happier than a person who's paid great but hates his or her job. But honestly, work is work and you're not always going to love your job. Even positions we feel blessed to have will irk us sometimes, give us headaches, and possibly make us want to quit. You may be doing what you love in a position and still dislike certain aspects of your job. That's life and that's work. If you start your dream job thinking it's going to be absolutely perfect, you'll lose the excitement and commitment you had for it when all of your expectations aren't met.

Myth #4: Workplace Racism Doesn't Exist Anymore: This sounds like a blatant lie to most working African-Americans, but some do believe this myth. They cling on to the fantasy that true equality really does exist in every workplace, even though they've seen statistics showing otherwise, and have heard some of their relatives or friends talk about how they've been treated unfairly or differently because of their skin color. But until they've felt the sting of workplace racism, they'll always hold this unrealistic belief. It's true that workplace racism is not as blatant as it was 40 or even 20 years ago. It's also true that African-Americans and other minorities have more opportunities than ever before. But it's unwise to think that everyone will judge you based on your character. Discrimination takes place throughout America on a daily basis—from people not hiring someone because of their ethnicity, to people treating someone differently once they are hired because of their ethnicity. If you believe otherwise, you'll think it's just your bad luck if you get passed over for multiple promotions you deserved, are getting paid far less than everyone else, and are stuck with menial work on the job that no one else has to do. Just because you've never been called the "n" word at work doesn't mean that workplace racism is a thing of the past.

Myth #5: Workplace Sexism Doesn't Exist Anymore: Just because Oprah's kicking butt and taking names in her industry doesn't mean that everyone is going to appreciate and welcome a strong sista in the one you're in. We live and work in a male-dominated society. Some of these men really do believe we can't or shouldn't compete with them in the workplace, and will let us know this bluntly or on the sly. Don't get duped into believing that all men see you as their equal.

Chapter 10

Evaluating Job Offers

"Failure to recognize opportunities is the most dangerous and common mistake one can make."
—Mae Jemison

Of course you want to make the right choice. You didn't come this far to get stuck with a low paying job or one that doesn't challenge you. You want a salary your mom's eyes will widen over, a benefits package your friends wish they had, perks to die for, a boss who has your back, and co-workers who want to see you succeed. Okay, it would be fantastic to have all of those things, but more than anything you want to know that the chair you're sitting in at work is the chair you're meant to be in.

Well, unless you're given a pretty good sign, you'll need faith, intuition and research on the company whose offer you're evaluating in order to make a wise decision. Even though times can get rough and sometimes working anywhere may seem fine to you, you still should analyze any and all job offers. Not all jobs are worth taking. Making the right decision becomes even more important when you're considering moving away to take a position, not going back to school, or taking a professional position that really doesn't fall in line with your career goals. Consider

the following when evaluating a company and its job offer:
1. The Industry
    - History of growth
    - Predictable future need for goods and services
    - Degrees of dependence on business trends
2. The Organization
    - Prestige and reputation
    - Growth potential
    - Size
    - Financial stability
    - Quality of management team
3. The Job
    - Training program
    - Day-to day activities
    - Amount of stress/pressure
    - Requirements to relocate, travel
    - Requirements to work long hours/weekends
    - Responsibility/autonomy
    - Opportunity for advancement
    - Salary
    - Benefits package
    - Involvement with supervisor, peer associates
    - Physical work environment
    - Social significance of work
    - Pace of work
    - Opportunity for continuing education/training
4. General Lifestyle
    - Your comfort with the organization's goals and philosophy
    - Geographic location
    - Recreational, cultural and educational facilities
    - Proximity of educational institutions for further study

From the Job Search Handbook of the University of North Carolina at Chapel Hill, copyright holder; used with permission.

OTHER IMPORTANT FACTORS TO CONSIDER

- The number of African-Americans and other minorities present and the primary positions they hold (entry level, middle management, management).
- The female-to-male ratio and the primary positions women hold (entry level, middle management, management).
- What is deemed professional and unprofessional as far as styles of dress, hairstyles and jewelry. Some companies may demand that you come to work in a business suit everyday. Other companies may consider your khari shell necklace, braids, or short cropped natural hairstyle as unprofessional.

It's good to get other people's opinions on the job offers you receive, but the final choice will be yours. People determine how good a job offer is according to their own values and goals, and you must do the same. What is worth more to you? Money? Peace? Excellent benefits and perks? Challenging work? Do you want the chance to rise in the ranks, or do you really just want something that will keep you busy and provide a steady paycheck? There's no wrong or right answer, just think about the kind of person you are and the type of environment you will be comfortable in. A person who hates working in teams will probably despise a job that requires them to work on a lot of team projects. Someone who has no sense of time doesn't need to be in a deadline-driven environment. An ambitious sista has no place in a company that hardly ever promotes from within. Also consider your gut feeling about the company. You know, the little voice that says there's something funny going on with this company, or you and your potential boss probably won't get along.

I used to ignore my gut feelings about people or a company I might be working for because I was so happy to be offered a job. Would-be supervisors would give me all the hints I needed that they would make my workday miserable, or the company was run poorly, but I would always think, "Well, I really need a job." In one instance, everyone from the company's recruiter to its secretary warned me that the boss I was about to work for was one horn away from being a devil. I took the job anyway. Two months and 30 headaches later I was looking for another job. Now if I get any sense that a job I take will leave me praying for quitting time every day—because of my duties, boss, or co-workers—I won't take it.

After your interview, reflect on your initial thoughts about the company. What positive aspects of the company stood out? What did you find odd? Did you feel like you wouldn't fit in right after you met the person who may become your boss? Did the employees look or act like the last people you'd want to work with, or did they make you want to start work with them off-the-clock? You should take all these issues into consideration when you're evaluating a job offer.

Chapter 11

Understanding Company Benefits

"Everything that can be counted does not necessarily count; everything that counts cannot necessarily be counted."
—Albert Einstein

When you tell someone you've been offered a position you're bound to be asked two very important questions: what's the salary and what are the benefits. Yet, while many people tune in when an employer talks about the paycheck they'll bring home, many also tune out the employer when they start discussing the benefits. This is usually because they're calculating what they can buy with the money they're offered, or don't know the importance of employee benefits.

Employee benefits are items of compensation that are given to an employee in addition to a salary. Whether or not an employer offers a benefits package and the extent of their offering is often a major determining factor in whether someone will accept a job. Most established medium-sized to large companies will offer their employees some type of benefits package; startups or those with only a handful of employees may not because they lack the capital. Usually only full-time employees are eligible for benefits. When applying for jobs and choosing between jobs, pay careful attention to the benefits package an employer offers. Think carefully about choosing a job that only offers a salary.

VARIOUS EMPLOYEE BENEFITS

Health Insurance: Health insurance is by far the most important benefit an employer can offer. When companies offer health insurance they either pay your entire monthly premium themselves or pay a portion of your premium. Either way can save you a tremendous amount of money. The monthly cost of health insurance for a young non-smoking female can range anywhere from $75 to $200 a month—a lot of money to pay on your own. Health insurance plans cover many services, including hospital, medical, dental, vision, and mental health services. Employers are also able to offer disability, life, and long-term care insurance.

401(k) Plan: 401(k) plans can offer you an early start to a comfortable retirement. The plan allows a portion of your salary and the income tax that would have been paid on that amount to be set aside for your retirement. Employers often match the amount you put in your 401(k).

Paid Annual/Vacation Leave: Paid annual/vacation leave is the number of days per year that you may take off for any reason. The number of days is usually determined by the length of time one has worked for the company. Many companies that offer annual/vacation leave require a person to work for a full year before they can receive this benefit.

Paid Sick Leave: Sick leave days are used when you are unable to work for health reasons. Sick leave normally accrues on a weekly or monthly basis.

Paid Family Sick Leave: This type of sick leave allows you to take time off from work to care for a sick immediate family member.

Maternity Leave: This allows women, and sometimes men, to take a leave of absence for the birth of their child and for the caring of their child shortly after the baby is born. Some employers offer maternity leave until the early infancy of the child. Employers may or may not pay a woman her monthly salary while she is on maternity leave, but they do hold her position at the company.

Other benefits offered by employers

Stock Options: Employees are given stocks in the company they work for or are offered them at a discounted price. Sometimes companies match the number of stocks an employee buys.

Educational: The employer may pay a portion or all of the cost for work related coursework and degree programs.

Professional Development: The employer may pay the cost of work related workshops, seminars, conferences and any training that will provide you with more knowledge in your field.

Child Care: The employer pays some or all of the cost of child care or offers onsite child care facilities.

Travel: The employer pays for business related travel expenses such as airfair, accommodations, car rentals and meals.

Employee Discounts: The employer provides discounts or waives fees on the products or services the company offers. For example, many people who work for airlines are able to fly for free, and retail employees can usually expect a discount off the company's merchandise.

Which job would you choose in the following scenario?

You are looking for an entry-level caseworker position with a reputable organization in Austin, Texas that pays at least $27,000 per year. You would prefer that they have a diverse staff, make a point of promoting from within, and offer you your own office because you don't like the idea of sharing your space with someone else.

Company A fits most of your criteria but only offers you a starting salary of $26,000. This, however, includes fully paid health and life insurance, paid sick leave, a two-week paid vacation, and the company will also pay for half the cost for you to receive a master's degree in a program geared towards people in your field.

Company B offers you a starting salary of $30,000, but tells you they will be unable to offer you any benefits. They do, however, offer a two-week unpaid vacation.

Which company sounds good to you? When looking just at the salary, it is easy to say that one should choose Company B. Yet, after looking at Company B's lack of benefits you might change your mind. The difference in salary is somewhat wide, but the benefits Company A offers overcompensates for the lower salary.

Company A will pay the full cost of health insurance. If you had to pay $100 a month for your own health insurance that would cost you $1,200 a year. They also offer life insurance, which you probably don't think you need. But still, if you paid for it at only $25 a month that would cost you $300 per year. After working there a year, Company A gives you a two-week paid vacation. Company B offers a two-week unpaid vacation, which means you would lose out on roughly $1,083. Finally, Company A offers to pay half of your graduate expenses. If the cost was just $15,000 a year, Company A would save you $7,500.

So, though the salary Company A offers is $4,000 less than

Company B, it will provide you with more than $10,083 in benefits.

Under some circumstances, however, it would make more sense to choose Company B, which might include:
- If you only planned on working there a year or two.
- If you were covered under someone else's health insurance plan.
- If you did not plan on attending graduate school or wanted a master's degree in another field.

As you can see, benefits are a major part of the compensation an employer offers you. Always keep in mind your needs and goals to help you make the best decision.

Chapter 12

Choosing Between Jobs

*"It's not hard to make decisions when
you know what your values are."*
—Roy Disney

If you get the chance to choose between jobs consider yourself lucky—many people wait and wait for just one job offer. Sometimes it will be easy to decide which job to take. But choosing the right job can become much harder when you must make a choice between equally desirable positions. A simple way to pick the job that will best meet your needs is by using a rating sheet. With a rating sheet you'll write down the work features that are most important to you at a company, and then rate each one according to those features on a scale of one to five (1=poor/5=excellent).

Using this job rating method allows you to see the big picture, as you're able to take everything into consideration. You shouldn't choose a job solely because of its salary, benefits, or any other single feature. Everything the job offers and doesn't offer should be taken into consideration. How long will you stay with a high paying company if it's in a city that makes you weary? What good is a three-week paid vacation if you don't make enough money to go out of the city? Think on these things as you make your decision. The company that scores the highest is probably your best bet.

SAMPLE RATING SHEET FOR THREE JOB OFFERS

Work Feature	Comp. A	Comp. B	Comp. C
◆ Salary	4	4	3
◆ Challenging work	2	5	3
◆ Great location	5	3	3
◆ Size of company	1	4	2
◆ Minimal supervision	1	3	5
◆ Travel	1	1	1
◆ Work environment	4	4	3
◆ Diverse workplace	2	4	2
◆ Room to advance	3	3	3
◆ Benefits	5	5	5
◆ Vacation time	5	5	5
◆ Tuition reimbursement	1	5	5
	Comp. A: 34	Comp. B: 46	Comp. C: 40

Accepting a Job Offer

When you're sure that you've made the best choice given your options, enthusiastically accept the job offer you've chosen. You may accept the offer over the phone, but you should also follow it up in writing. Thank them for the offer and confirm the terms of the offer (starting date, salary, benefits). Concisely summarize what impressed you most about the position/company, and close by saying that you look forward to joining the company.

Rejecting a Job Offer

Once you've decided which job you want to take, you should reject every offer you received graciously, either by phone or in writing. One day you may want to work for the company and you'll be more likely to receive another job offer if you left a good impression.

Chapter 13

Getting the Salary You Deserve

*"In business, you don't get what you deserve,
you get what you negotiate."*
—*Chester Karras*

Negotiating the salary for a particular position is an unfamiliar practice for a majority of recent college graduates. Many of us are used to just being told what the pay is for a position we've applied for and accepting it. This is largely because the positions we took in college and high school weren't professional positions so we didn't expect to receive much; we were just happy to have a job. But when it comes to the type of "real money" we're hoping to make in the real world we can't leave the salary we're going to receive up to chance. After all, this is the money we will have to live off of.

If your goal is to get the highest possible salary that you can for a position then you'll have to know how to negotiate for it. But before you can confidently negotiate your salary you should know what you should expect to be paid for your time and talent. The salary you should expect to receive is determined by a variety of factors, including:

- Your occupation.
- The demand within your field.
- Your experience.
- The city and state you reside in.
- The particular employer.

Before the interview you should do your research to find out what people in your field, with your education and experience are getting paid. Then you need to go further and determine how much the average person within your field, with your education and experience gets paid in the city you live in. If possible, it would be great to know the average salary employees with your job title make at the company you're trying to join.

After considering what your research reveals you then have to look at the salary being offered for the position you're applying for. Employers often give salary ranges for advertised positions, such as $25,000-$29,000, or $32,000-$40,000. The salary range for the position can help you come up with a figure before you're asked to. The important thing to remember is that your salary isn't carved in stone. Your earnings can and should be discussed to benefit you. However, you must also keep an open mind when trying to determine your asking price. Some positions are more negotiable than others.

You have more room to negotiate when:
- People with your occupation are in demand, and there are few skilled people.
- You have a high level of experience.
- You have special skills or talents.
- You have an advanced degree.

You have the least room to negotiate when:
- There's little demand for people with your occupation.
- There's a high demand for people in your field, but an over-abundance of skilled people.
- You have little experience.

- The position is entry-level.
- The employer is on an extremely tight budget.
- The employer determines salaries by a pay scale.
- You have an advanced degree, but not in the field you're trying to enter.

Let's Talk Money!

Most negotiation experts advise you to let the employer initiate questions about your salary expectations. When the employer does start asking salary related questions, take time to ask some also. Two very important questions are "What is the salary range for this position?" and "What would be the salary range for someone with my qualifications?" You can ask these questions even if you've already found out the answer from another source. The employer's answers to these questions can help you determine the amount of money he or she is considering offering you. With this information you can keep yourself from under pricing yourself and missing out on more money or overpricing yourself and not getting offered the job.

It's actually wiser to not ask for or agree to a specific figure until after you've been offered the position. An employer is more likely to give you your desired salary if they've already chosen you to fill the position. When asked about your salary requirements in an initial interview, you can give a salary range that you're willing to work with. You can say something like, "I'd expect to make somewhere between $30,000 to $37,000, but I'm sure we could come to an agreement at that time."

It's time to really talk money when you've been offered the position and the salary question is presented by the employer. But never just throw out any old number! The salary you ask for should depend on the information the employer gave you, what your research has revealed to be appropriate compensation, and your own realistic salary expectations.

During the salary negotiations you should practice the following rules:
- Ask for more than what you're really shooting for.
- Act like you deserve the salary, not like you need it.
- Be polite.
- Stress how much you want the position.

The key to getting the salary you desire is being able to convince the employer that you're worth every penny of it. If you're lucky, your asking price will be acceptable to the employer and you won't have to play the money game. If the figure isn't what the employer had in mind then you'll have to do your best to change his or her opinion. This is where your research will come in handy. When you're trying to negotiate a higher figure than what you've been offered, or the employer says your asking price is too high, you can use the following reasons to support being given the salary you're aiming for:

1. Other companies are paying more: If other similar companies are paying more money to people with the same position then kindly enlighten the employer. "My research has shown that other medical assistants in New Orleans working for physicians in private practice make approximately the same wage I asked for. Because of this I feel that $15 an hour is appropriate and fair."

2. You have special talents/skills: If you have more to offer than just what the position calls for remind the employer of this. "I understand that $40,000 is more than the average entry-level accountant at your company is paid. However, as you told me earlier, you currently don't have any Spanish speaking accountants. I would be able to work with clients you've been having to turn away, thus producing more revenue for the company."

3. Your qualifications merit you more money: Don't get stuck with entry-level pay when you have experience. Politely remind the employer of your qualifications. "$35,000 seems a bit low for someone with my professional experience and education. I have worked as a graphic designer for three years and have a master's degree in graphic design. Based on this, I feel that I should receive a minimum of $50,000."

4. Your occupation is in demand: If you work in a field that has a lot of job openings but few skilled people to fill them, then remind the employer of this. "No, $40,000 doesn't seem like a lot to me considering how in-demand nurses are. There's a shortage of nurses in this area and many employers are offering $45,000 per year plus sign-on bonuses."

5. The position should obviously pay more: If they're offering you a salary that seems ridiculous considering your duties explain this to them in the nicest way possible. "I honestly believe that this public relations specialist position should pay more than $25,000, given the wide range of duties it comes with. If I understand correctly, this position requires someone to work in excess of 50 hours a week, help other departments with their projects, serve as a back-up administrative assistant to the director, and volunteer two weekends out of the month. I feel that a salary of $30,000 would be more fair and appropriate given the wide range of duties I would have."

6. You have other job offers: Tactfully let the employer know that you've been offered another job that pays the amount you're asking for or more. This shows the employer that you're in demand. "$42,000 is good, however, I've been offered $45,000 at another company. Is it possible for you to also offer $45,000?"

Salary Negotiation Techniques

The negotiation for your salary usually begins after the employer has done one of the following: 1) Offers you a specific figure; 2) Gives you his or her salary range; or 3) Avoids discussing the salary range for the position and asks you what your expectations are. Here's how to handle all three situations:

1. When Given A Specific Figure: If the employer gives you a specific figure it's likely for one of three reasons: They've already considered your qualifications and the amount given is what they feel you deserve; they pay according to a scale; or this is the amount they've budgeted for the position. If you're offered much more than you hoped for, your best bet would be to tell the employer that the amount is fair and in line with what you were expecting. If the figure is less than the amount you were shooting for then perhaps it's time to negotiate.

For example, Akia is being interviewed for an entry-level social worker position with a non-profit agency that she knows doesn't pay very well. She's determined that if offered the job she'll only take it if it pays at least $25,000 plus benefits. But of course she'd like more. Here's how she handled the salary negotiation.

Employer:	"Well Akia, the position pays $25,000 plus benefits.
Akia:	"Oh? Honestly Ms. Harper, I expected that this position would pay at least $28,000, given the duties you described and the degree required. In fact, my research has shown that the starting salary for the majority of entry-level social workers hired by non-profit agencies in Portland is approximately $28,000."
Employer:	"I know. However, we are on a really tight budget. Would $26,000 suffice?"
Akia:	"Actually, I'm shooting for at least $27,000 as a social worker. I really want to work here. You and your staff seem like you'd be wonder-

ful to work with, and I respect this organization for what its done to serve the community. But I won't feel like I'm fairly compensated with $26,000."

Employer: "Hmmmm. Okay. I think I can stretch the budget a little bit to get you in here. You'll be happy with $27,000?"

Akia: "Yes."

2. When given a salary range: If the employer gives you a salary range you should always ask for something at the high end of the range or at least more than you are expecting. This way, if the employer feels the figure is too high and offers you a lower salary, chances are that it'll still be more than you were expecting.

Here's how Shamia worked with the salary range given to her after being offered a job as an admissions counselor at a large university. She knows the salary range is $32,000-$38,000. She's hoping to start off at the high end of that range even though she'd be happy just to get the job and $32,000 a year.

Employer: "I'm very impressed with what you've accomplished thus far, Shamia. I'm sure you'll be a wonderful addition to our admissions staff and learn a lot working here. As you know, the salary range for the admissions counselor position is $32,000-$38,000, and the salary is commensurate with experience. What are your salary expectations?"

Shamia: "I'm certain I'll enjoy working here too! Thank you so much for offering me the position. Regarding my salary, I'd like to start off at $37,000. I know that a lower salary range

	would be reserved for someone with little or no experience. And although I've never worked as an admissions counselor, I did work for two years as the senior resident assistant at the university I attended. As I explained earlier, a large part of that role was advising students regarding their majors and class schedules."
Employer:	"I see. Actually, someone with your experience would probably start off at around $35,000. Individuals who have served five or more years as actual admissions counselors for a university would generally be the only ones offered more than $36,000. So, I'd be happy to offer you $35,000. And of course, you have to take into consideration that we offer an excellent benefits package."
Shamia:	"That's true, the university's benefits package is very good, and I know that admissions counselors come up for a pay raise every two years. But would it be possible for me to start off at $35,500?"
Employer:	"You know what? That's only $500 more. And you seem like you'll relate to the students very well. I can do that."

3. When Not Given a Salary Range: Some employers are tricky. They want to know exactly what you're expecting so they'll have the upperhand when it's time to talk about your salary. Of course, they're hoping the salary you ask for is lower than what they'd be willing to give you. When faced with this dilemma, all you have to base your decision on is the research you've done and the amount you're shooting for. If it's lower than what they would've offered you'll never know, but if it's too high you're sure to hear about it. When they feel it's a little up there all you can do is try to justify your figure with your research and what you feel is fair.

Let's look at how Tatyana handled herself when faced with this problem. She's at the salary negotiation stage of her interview for a math teaching position at a charter school. She's found that second year charter school teachers make about $28,000, far less than second year math teachers at public schools. Still, she'd like to start off at $31,000 or more.

Employer:	"It looks like you're our candidate of choice Tatyana. The only thing left to discuss is your salary. What are your salary expectations?"
Tatyana:	"If it's okay with you, I'd like to know the salary range you've designated for this position before I give a specific figure."
Employer:	"I don't have a salary range. The salary is commensurate with experience."
Tatyana:	"Then what do you feel would be appropriate for someone with my qualifications?"
Employer:	"I'm not sure. I'm pretty open. Just tell me what you're aiming for and I'll see what I can do."
Tatyana:	"Well, other charter school teachers I've talked to say that the average salary for a teacher with two years of experience should be a minimum of $32,000, and that's what I'm shooting for."
Employer:	"Really? Unfortunately, because we're grant

funded most of our teachers don't make over $31,000, and I really can't afford to pay you that much. I was thinking $29,000."

Tatyana: "I understand, but please keep in mind that there is a shortage of math teachers in this area, and I would also be volunteering my time to coach the girls' volleyball team. I really do want this job. I think this is a wonderful school and I want to be a part of it."

Employer: "I want you to be a part of this school too. But there's another candidate that I know will take the job if I offer her just $29,000."

Tatyana: "But she's not your candidate of choice." (she says smiling)

Employer: "Hmmmm. You got me there. Okay. Let me think........okay, I can offer you $31,000."

Tatyana: "I think that's fair. When do I start?"

Akia, Shamia and Tatyana all managed to secure a salary of at least $2,000 more than what they were shooting for or offered by following the salary negotiation rules. They asked for more than what they were really shooting for, acted like they deserved the salary (not like they needed it), they were polite, and they made it a point to stress how much they wanted the position.

Take It or Leave It?

Of course, you have to be prepared for salary negotiations that don't work out in your favor. An employer may not budge at all when you ask for a little more money. You'll basically be asked to take it or leave it. Only you can decide if the money is right.

Don't take an employer's unwillingness to pay you what you feel you deserve personally. They're operating from a totally different perspective than you, and they may feel you deserve the salary you desire but really can't fit it into their budget. Don't flat out refuse a job when you're asked to take it or leave it. Ask the employer if you can take a day to think about their offer, and then go home and consider your options. If you really need a job you can always take it and keep interviewing for other positions. You can also work a part-time job to bring in some extra money.

Just remember that the salary you start out with will help determine the salary you'll have throughout your career with the company, despite raises and promotions. If you start out feeling poorly compensated it's likely that you will never feel like you're earning what you deserve. Also, a future employer may base the salary they offer you on what you received at your former job. If you worked for peanuts at the company you left, they may expect for you to work for peanuts for them too.

Answering Salary Questions Before the Interview

Some employers will ask you to state the salary you desire for a position on your application or with the resume and cover letter you send in. This is often done to screen out candidates who don't fall within the salary range they've set. This poses two problems: You may over price yourself and not get an interview, or under price yourself and be locked into the salary you stated if offered the job. Because of this it's best to write that your salary is "negotiable" or "open" unless employers won't accept your application or resume without your salary requirement.

When you must write something put the minimum amount that you will work for, and state that you would like to receive a starting salary of *at least* whatever you've decided is the lowest amount (Ex: "I'd like to receive a starting salary of at least $48,000.") Writing "at least" keeps you from locking yourself into a specific figure if hired, and positions you to ask for more.

Chapter 14

Meeting & Exceeding Your Employer's Expectations

*"Here is a simple but powerful rule:
always give people more than what they expect to get."*
—Nelson Boswell

As a college student you pretty much knew what your professors expected of you. You were told to show up on time ready to learn, and to try your best to make A's in your classes, or to at least pass them. If only things were that simple in the real world. During your first few weeks or perhaps months on the job you may feel like a freshman again—very unsure of how you're going to succeed in this new environment. This feeling normally stems from just not knowing what you must do to perform well. This can be complicated by the fact that some employers may not be as straightforward as your former professors about what they desire of you. Sure, you know you're supposed to come to work on time, but what else? What will set you apart from your other co-workers? What will ensure that you get promotions? What will keep your boss happy and out of your way?

I have had a lot of bosses because I started working when I was 14, and have temped through employment agencies. Some bosses, like the project manager I did educational research for, gave me some pointers and then expected me to figure out most things by myself. That worked great for me, but only because she was not very demanding or critical. However, when I worked briefly as a publicist's assistant, my boss gave me the same leeway and I failed miserably. Every other day she would ask me why I hadn't done something that I didn't know I was supposed to do—like calling her when I got back from lunch or checking to see if she needed anything throughout the day. After two weeks, I politely asked her if she could write down all the small nuances of the position that were not discussed during the interview. This way, I explained, I could ensure I was performing my job to her satisfaction. After she emailed me her two-page list she never had to ask me why I hadn't done something again.

One of the first objectives I now give myself when starting a new job is to find out exactly what my boss expects of me and what makes my boss tick (positively and negatively). It's important that you make this an objective as well. Employers don't give out A's B's or C's, but they definitely grade you. You might be able to find out what your employer expects of you by just asking. Some employers will be able to tell you all of their expectations, right down to not taking a personal call longer than five minutes. But others might not be able to put all of their expectations into words. That's why you should be aware of some general expectations that most employers have.

Your Employer Expects and Wants You to Be:

- *A Team Player:* An employee who is able to relate and work well with a diverse group of people. Someone who leaves his or her problems at the front door, and shows up to work with a "winning" attitude. A person who can pull his or her own load and doesn't gripe about having to pull someone else's at times.

- *A Go-Getter:* An employee who can get the ball rolling alone. Someone who doesn't have to be babied or asked twice to do something. A person who can generate new ideas and actually benefit the company.

- *Multifaceted:* An employee whose skills aren't limited to those needed just for his or her specific position. Someone who can perform a variety of duties with ease and enthusiasm, and is willing to learn new skills.

- *Flexible:* An employee who can "go with the flow," and handle assignments as needed. Someone who won't say things like "There's no way I can work those hours," "I didn't plan on and don't want to work on this assignment," or "I can't believe I have to share an office with three people."

- *A Good Communicator:* An employee with poise, tact, and something worthwhile to say. Someone with a good command of the English language that can converse with ease. An employee who can also write as compellingly as they speak.

You may not naturally possess all of these qualities, but luckily these are all qualities that you can work on. Not many people are able to walk into their new work environment and blow everyone's mind. And relax, because for the most part no one expects you to. Your employer and fellow co-workers probably know that you haven't been working professionally for long, and hopefully they understand that you have a lot to learn. They were anxious and uncertain about how well they would do too. In fact, they still are. People always have to live up to another person's expectations at work. Your main focus should be on doing your job and doing it well.

Now that you know what qualities are crucial for you to possess, you can go about learning what unique expectations your employer has. And some can be very "unique."

I had a manager who expected me and other employees working on a project to keep her updated on our work every 30 minutes via a phone call (I am not making this up). She asked this even though she was able to go into her computer system and actually see what we had each completed and when.

After making the mistake of believing another manager when she said, "Please feel free to come to me with any and all questions," I soon learned through her huffs and puffs that she really meant, "If you can't find anyone else to help you then ask me, but make it quick." I began acting as nonverbally directed.

My co-workers have always been my best resource for information on how to do well at a company. Most times I did not have to ask. People were more than willing to tell me all of the boss's pet peeves, as well how to get on his or her good side.

As you attempt to meet and exceed your employer's expectations, you're going to grow in more ways than one. You'll be a better team player, go-getter, communicator, multifaceted, and flexible person than you ever thought you could be in college. You'll also, hopefully, be a model employee—the kind that your boss will have another rookie talk to when he or she asks, "What do you expect from me?"

Chapter 15

Fitting In as the New Girl at Work

"You can observe a lot by watching."
—Yogi Berra

Being the new girl on the job can feel like being the new girl at school. You want to fit in and be liked by your co-workers (the students) and your boss (the teacher) while feeling at home in your new environment.

One of the key ways to fit in is by understanding and adapting to the company's culture. Just as every school you attended had its own way of life and culture, so will all the companies you work for throughout your life. You'll find that every company operates differently—has its own quirky way of doing things and rules that reflect the beliefs of the higher-ups. You may find that some companies will take some getting used to while others will automatically feel welcoming and safe. How fast you learn to operate within your company's culture will dictate how fast you'll fit into the company itself.

This is not to say that you can't stand apart from your co-workers in your own unique way, and do things a little differently. What this means is that there are certain aspects of a company that you'll have to adapt to. It's rare to find a company whose atmosphere is entirely suitable to you. There may always be something you wish were different, or done differently. You'll find that some things can be changed by your insightful suggestions. Other quirky aspects of the company will be unchangeable, and that's okay if you can accept what can't be changed.

The following are seven characteristics that I've found work together to create a company's culture.

1. The Employer's Expectations: Each employer has his or her own expectations for the company. The employees pick up on these expectations and carry themselves accordingly (or should). Some employers may expect their company to just get by and make a little profit. You'll be able to tell this because your co-workers will do just what it takes to get by and collect a paycheck. While you should still strive for excellence you won't be able to condemn others for their lack of initiative in this type of environment. Other employers will want their company to be the best in the city, state or nation, and be very demanding of their employees. Half-stepping on your job in this company will be frowned upon.

2. The Rules and Regulations: Each company will have their own set of do's and don'ts to work by. Rules like stealing, backtalking the boss, lying and so forth are no-brainer rules, but others might not be so obvious. You may not find out exactly what they are until you break a rule or see someone getting fussed at for committing a "no-no." For example, some companies may not have a problem with employees relaxing on the job when the workload is slow. Other companies may expect you to look like you're working even when they know there's nothing to do. Likewise, dating among employees is a normal occurrence at some companies, while it may be forbidden at others. To avoid confusion, ask whether or not something is against company policy or considered an "abomination" before you do something you're unsure about.

3. The Interaction Among Co-workers: If you find that people rarely leave their cubicles and like to eat lunch alone at your company, then being Miss Friendly might not score you any points. This isn't to say don't be upbeat and cordial, but don't be upset if other people aren't as amiable as you are. Other companies may be under a heavy spirit of camaraderie that most people wish their company had. In this environment you'll hear people's gossip on your first day and be invited over for dinner the next. This is cool—if you appreciate friendly co-workers. If you don't, you better pretend you do and work on being friendly yourself if you want to fit in.

4. The Employee's Interaction With Management: There's a big difference in the atmosphere of a company where the boss is viewed as a team member, and one where he or she is solely looked upon as the head honcho. A team member boss may be treated casually by employees and joked with like anyone else. You can tell when you have a head honcho boss because the room will get quiet when he or she enters. Personal interaction with these two types of bosses is also very different. The team member boss might have what's known as an "open-door" policy where you can freely share your thoughts and concerns at any time. The head honcho boss may make you set an appointment to talk, and that may be the first and only time you get to talk to him or her one-on-one. Take cues from your co-workers on how to interact with your boss until you get to know his or her management style.

5. The Dress Code: Don't expect to fit in wearing business casual outfits when the atmosphere is conservative and everyone sports a suit except on Fridays. Take your cues on appropriate attire from your co-workers and follow their lead.

6. The Pace: If it's a fast-paced, deadline-driven environment you're working in, then you better keep up or you'll be seen as a dead weight. If it's a slower paced "take your time" environment then you might not fit in playing Speedy Gonzalez.

7. The Competitiveness: Some companies foster a competitive environment among employees. At companies like this your coworkers will gloat about who sold the most ads, who sold the most merchandise, which team bagged the most clients and finished the project first, and so on. If you're not a competitive person by nature this may take some getting used to.

Chapter 16

Building & Maintaining a Positive Image

*"The way to gain a good reputation
is to endeavor to be what you desire to appear."*
—Socrates

Building and maintaining a positive image is as important in the real world as it was in college. The only difference is that the stakes are higher now if you get stuck with a bad reputation.

Word can travel fast about the good you do and the bad—the excellent image you project and the one that will keep you from advancing in your career. As African-American women we often have to struggle harder than our white counterparts to be respected and taken seriously; we don't want our own mistakes to be the cause of this.

Projecting an image that demands respect and developing a reputation as a diligent, intelligent and honest person should be considered an ongoing process for all of us. In order for us to succeed in the workplace and our careers we must be perceived in a positive light by our peers and the person who signs our paycheck. Though it's easy to forget, you must remember that everything you do and don't do, say and don't say, is picked apart and judged by others. People view your talk, your walk, your style of dress, and the overall way you carry yourself as a reflection of who you are and what you have to offer.

At this point in our lives we should have all been exposed to various types of questionable people one can find in almost any work environment: bossy people, manipulative people, brown-nosers, etc. It would be awful for you to be stereotyped on the job as "being" a certain way. And when it comes to black women, there are unfortunately some behavioral types that people think belong just to us. Please do all that you can to ensure you aren't labeled as being like one of these women:

Ms. That's Not My Job

"That's not my job" is her motto, but the real problem is that no one can figure out what she does anyway. All her peers wonder why she hasn't been fired yet and resent her because she doesn't pull her own weight. The word "teamwork" is not in her dictionary, and neither is "diligence" and "competence." Ms. That's Not My Job spends most of her day pretending to work and thinking about what she's going to do with her next paycheck. She sees her job as just a stepping-stone to something greater, so she never really puts much effort into anything she does. When she gets passed up for promotions or fired she thinks it's because she didn't brown-nose the boss or because he or she just didn't like her.

Ms. Donna Karan

Her co-workers wonder if she's selling drugs or has a sugar daddy because they know she doesn't earn enough to sport all those expensive clothes. It's like this woman comes to work for the sole purpose of working her outfit. Everything she wears has its designer label in plain view and she'll find some way to tell you how much the outfit cost her. And while she can name every hot fashion designer in the industry and tell you when a new line is coming out, she draws a blank when you ask her anything about her industry and line of work. She doesn't realize that clothes don't make the woman and she'll never make it out of a cubicle with her present mindset.

Ms. Saved

Her peers are all out of excuses for why they can't go to church with her this week. It's not because they're heathens—they're actually afraid they'll get struck down in the church if they go with her. Ms. Saved put all her old ways behind her when she turned her life over to God except lying, gossiping, coveting thy neighbor's possessions and swearing when she thinks no one is listening. What's even more unacceptable is that she walks around acting like she's the salt of the earth and as if everyone but her needs to get their life together. When she's not quoting scriptures she's giving someone advice they didn't ask for. No boss will ever put her in a position of authority because her co-workers feel uneasy working with her. When she quits or gets fired from her job she'll tell the new person interviewing her that the people on her old job couldn't accept true Christians.

Ms. Too Damn Loud

Ms. Too Damn Loud's black co-workers wish they could slap her mouth shut, especially if they're in a predominantly white workplace, because they feel like she makes them all look bad. She is rude, loud, obnoxious, clumsy, and thinks that "keepin' it real" means telling anyone who so much as looks at her funny where they can go. Ms. Too Damn Loud criticizes other black women and men who have a quieter demeanor, whispering to her other loud friends that he or she is "just trying to be white." She is quick to label white people as racists and black people as sell-outs when they tell her that her loudness and over aggressiveness is unbefitting of a professional and she needs to start looking for another job.

Ms. Booty Call

Men's eyes widen and jaws drop when they see Ms. Booty Call approaching. She looks like she is auditioning for a Lil' Jon video with her booty-hugging pants, cleavage baring shirts, caked on make-up, break your ankle high-heels, witch-like fingernails, and head full of weave. She purposefully draws too much attention to herself but still tells her female co-workers to "stop hating." She tricked the person interviewing her into offering her a job by wearing a three-piece suit, but now she thinks her job at work is to sit back and look cute. Ms. Booty Call wouldn't last long in Burger King, much less in a professional environment. If she doesn't make a dramatic change in her appearance her career will be ruined.

Ms. Congeniality

Everyone in the office loves her and doesn't know what they would do without her, which is probably because she does everything. She is the nicest person anyone could work with, but she's just too nice. Ms. Congeniality gives turning the other cheek a whole new meaning, and people take advantage of her timidness and sweet nature. Because she is afraid of being disliked she never questions anyone or anything. Because she is afraid to ask for what she wants (like a raise or promotion), she'll likely stay stuck in the same position making the same amount of money she did when she got hired five years ago.

Ms. Hypochondriac

There is always something wrong with this woman and nothing is ever okay with her. She would complain about winning the lottery if she hit the right numbers. She's the one in the office meeting that asks 10 repetitive questions that no one cares about, and complains about things that most people wouldn't think twice about. Someone babied her too much in her childhood and now she expects to get everything her way or she throws a temper tantrum. Besides being a nag, she's also prone to being a tattle-tale. When people aren't trying to avoid her they're tuning out everything she says. Despite the fact that people have told her she complains too much, she still can't figure out why no one gets along with her and why her employer said the company can no longer afford to keep her.

Ms. Praying Mantis

Ms. Praying Mantis intimidates everyone, including her boss. Her drive, intelligence and hard work have made her very successful, but she is not well liked because of her attitude. She acts like she has something to prove to everyone and people generally know to stay out of her way. She's taken the "strong, beautiful, black woman" thing to another level and is in a league of her own because she's alienated most of her peers. Her boss won't fire her because she's an excellent worker, but unless she calms down and realizes that she can get ahead without biting off people's heads, she'll never be where she really wants to be.

Ms. Back-stabbing Crab

Ms. Back-stabbing Crab gives sistas a bad name. She "smiles in your face, while all the time trying to take your place." While Ms. Praying Mantis is intimidating, this woman is downright treacherous and there's no one she dislikes more than other successful black women and men. Insecure and jealous, she tries to sabotage and bring down other black people who are doing better than her or trying to get to where she is. She makes the work environment resemble a battlefield and aims straight for people's reputations by lying about and setting traps for those she feels are out of line. Because she's sneaky and smart it sometimes takes a little too long for her superiors to catch on to her, but when her claws are discovered she'll find herself in the bottom of the barrel.

Ms. You've Got To Be Kidding

"You've got to be kidding," is what the person interviewing this woman said when she walked through the door. Her make-up was all jacked up, her clothes were wrinkled and very out of style, and she may have forgotten to comb her hair. Still, she had impeccable credentials so she got hired. Now she's on the job and both women and men try to hint that she may want to get a make-over if she expects the boss to let her meet and greet customers. People just can't figure out how she can be so smart but not see that the way she dresses and keeps herself is preventing her from getting ahead. If she takes just a few tips from Ms. Donna Karan (who talks about her behind her back), she will go further at her company and in life.

Ms. Low Self

Ms. Low Self is hard-working and extremely smart. Her only problem is that she has very low self-esteem, which doesn't make sense because the girl has it going on. However, because she thinks so lowly of herself she constantly criticizes herself in front of others, doesn't share her ideas in fear of being rejected, and she never really takes credit for her accomplishments because she thinks they happened by luck. Her self-defeating actions keep her from truly being valued at her company and moving up.

As you can see, these are women you don't want to emulate. Furthermore, you shouldn't even hang around some of these women. Of course, on the more positive end of the spectrum are black women that make you very proud, and question how you can get on their level. Ms. Now That's What I'm Talking About embodies these women.

Ms. Now That's What I'm Talking About

She has everyone's attention from the moment she steps into a room. Men are in awe of her because she possesses both beauty and brains. Women can't help but feel a tinge of jealousy because she looks and acts like she has everything together. She is an employer's dream—a poised, confident, cordial, hard working, dedicated employee who does more than just get the job done: she checks her attitude at the door, and no matter how much her boss and co-workers ruffle her feathers she's yet to break a sweat. Ms. Now That's What I'm Talking About will succeed whether she is trying to climb the corporate ladder or thrive in a small business because she recognizes that image is everything.

The catch is that you can't just wake up one day and become Ms. Now That's What I'm Talking About. You have to work on becoming her.

Becoming Ms. Now That's What I'm Talking About

Critically analyze the image you're projecting: Most of us know the negative behaviors we need to work on, but we make excuses for trying not to change. I, for example, am much too open with people. If I'm in the right mood and I feel particularly comfortable, I could share my entire life story with a person I just met. While I generally like that I have such an easygoing personality, I have to remember that there is a thin line between being easygoing and unprofessional. I don't want to appear ditzy in the workplace and become labeled as someone who tells all of her business.

You should consider your personality and traits you have that could possibly annoy, anger or make people feel sorry for you. Do you tend to run off at the mouth and constantly find people telling you they'd love to chat with you a little longer but they have to get back to work? Are you somewhat absentminded and are frequently reminded by your co-workers and boss about assignments or tasks they are afraid you might forget? Do you try to get away with wearing casual clothing when your company's rules explicitly say to wear business casual attire or that is what the majority of people in your office wear? Unless you're totally clueless, you should be aware of at least some of the things you must work on to sharpen your image.

Ask someone you trust about what you can do to sharpen your image: Talk to someone you feel comfortable confiding in about how you want to maintain a professional image. Ask them if there is anything about your personality that might make others think negatively about you. Ask them to be truthful with you, and resist the urge to counter anything they say with an explanation as to why you behave a certain way.

Take notes from people you admire: Carefully watch how the most respected people at your company carry themselves. The type of people who are most respected differs from company to company. At some places, people who are strictly about business and act like workaholics are deemed the perfect employees. At other companies people with open, warm and outgoing personalities repeatedly win "Employee of the Week." Pick out people who are generally liked and admired and take a mental note of everything they do and don't do that wins the approval of others. If there are certain things a person does that you can easily add into your routine, such as making a point to always speak to people, then do them also. If some things are a little bit harder, such as dressing immaculately, but will really give your image a boost, then try, try and try some more to emulate that person.

Once you have identified the areas you want to work on you should write them down. I suggest writing a sentence on two sticky notes, such as "I will avoid gossiping and surfing the internet while I'm at work," or "I will avoid giving unconstructive criticism and being snappy when I'm in a bad mood." Put one sticky note inside your desk drawer at work and the other on your bathroom mirror so that you will see the sentences often. Then really try to work on improving in your problem areas.

Chapter 17

Managing Your Boss

"The most important single ingredient in the formula of success is knowing how to get along with people."
—*Theodore Roosevelt*

I always despised the word "boss." It sounded so controlling, so weighty, so self-important, so . . . bossy. Needless to say, I never liked the idea of having a boss either. That's why I always tried to choose jobs that gave me a high level of autonomy. But it was always clear to me that unless you own your own business, there is no way around having someone who plays the role of a boss. So through trial and error, I learned how to get along with my bosses. And when I saw that just "getting along" with my bosses wasn't exactly the smartest thing to do, I started learning how to "manage them." And I'm still learning.

A ton of books have been written on the sole subject of managing your boss. From *What Makes Bosses Tick and How You Can Cope With Them* to *Bosses from Hell: True Tales from the Trenches*, there are bookstore and library shelves stacked with reading material dedicated to these people. It's funny that thousands of pages could be written on one aspect pertaining to a person's working life. Yet, there is a reason for this anomaly.

Beyond being the individual that let's you get your foot in the door, your boss also determines what happens to you once the door closes. Whether you get a raise, important assignments, move up in the company, and sometimes whether you're able to move on to bigger and better things, is to a large extent determined by the person you answer to first thing in the morning.

You can't afford to look at your bosses as nuisances anymore—tolerating them as you may have during positions you held in college. Your boss is now someone you have to pay attention to. More importantly, your boss is now someone you have to manage.

An entire book may not be needed to key you in on how to interact and deal with your supervisors, but everyone starting out in their career can benefit from some pointers. The following advice is devised to help you manage those strange people we call bosses, and to help your career in the process.

DON'T GET CAUGHT SLIPPING

No matter how cool certain supervisors are, and no matter how chummy you are with them, you can be sure of two things: they know who's in charge and they're watching you. They're grading you in fact. Don't let them catch you slipping. When your boss thinks of you, you want him or her to think about how wise they were to hire you and what an asset you've been to the company. You help create and sustain this good picture through two ways: your performance on the job and the way you treat your boss. Think about it. You can't succeed at a company if you're a great employee but your boss hates you. And you can't succeed if you're a dead weight but loved by your boss. Your boss has to love you and your work. The following are ways to get your boss to do both.

Loving Your Work

Do Things Before They Are Asked Of You: It's one thing to do what your boss asks you to, it's quite another to have something done before you're even approached about it. Completing assignments or little tasks you know need to be done without being asked to makes you look industrious, thoughtful, and hardworking.

Volunteer For Extra Assignments: Bosses give extra credit just like teachers. You can earn extra credit from your boss by doing more than what's asked of you. Take on additional assignments when you have the time. This shows your commitment to the company and your enthusiasm.

Do Your Best All The Time: Don't just do your best on assignments you feel matter the most. Treat every assignment, from filing papers to entertaining notable clients, as important. Your boss won't feel comfortable letting you work on major assignments if you act like you can't or don't want to handle the simpler ones.

Bring Ideas To The Table: Present yourself as knowledgeable, creative and proactive by offering your boss suggestions and solutions. Don't wait to be asked what you think about something. If you have an idea that can benefit your company and boss then say so. Your boss will then think more highly of you, ask your opinion more often, and hopefully come to rely on you for help when problems arise.

Help Others: Don't lose out on an opportunity to help other employees by offering advice or training them. This demonstrates your team-player mentality and management skills while also showing that you're not out to just better yourself.

Loving You

Compliment Your Boss: Please note that the word was "compliment," not "kiss up." The difference is that one is sincere and the other is not. Your boss knows the difference. If you like their hairstyle, outfit, car, presentation or newly decorated office then say so. Everyone likes and remembers compliments, and your boss will like and remember all of yours.

Make Your Boss Look Good In Front Of His or Her Boss: A surefire way to gain your boss' approval is by telling that person's boss how much you admire his or her work ethic or other positive traits. By relating how much you like your boss, how hardworking or innovative he or she is, you demonstrate your loyalty and gain more brownie points than you can count.

Be Honest: Bosses, like everyone else, despise liars; don't let your boss catch you in a lie! You should be recognized as a person who's honest and sincere. When your boss asks your opinion state your thoughts truthfully and tactfully, even if you disagree with him or her. Don't just tell your boss what you think he or she wants to hear. Your boss will appreciate your honesty and trust you more.

Act Enthusiastic: Smile when you arrive to work. Act like you're glad to be alive and glad to have a job. You don't have to run around with a fake smile on your face 24/7, but you should definitely not sport a frown and constant yawn. You want your boss to feel like you enjoy your work and like working with him or her, not like you're at work just for the money and have to tolerate your boss (even if that's the truth). Acting enthusiastic makes your boss feel likable and in turn will make him or her treat you well.

Try practicing those tactics to create a better working relationship with your boss, and anyone else you have to report to. After working with your boss for a while you should be able to devise some of your own original tactics. To do this pay attention to what your boss considers both good and unprofessional work. Take note of the employees your boss seems to favor and dislike. In general, just find out what makes your boss tick.

SWIMMING WITH THE SHARKS

If you're lucky, you'll be blessed with a string of bosses that want to see you succeed and will do everything they can to help you. You'll find that these bosses require little management. They also, however, are rare.

If you're like the majority of working Americans you'll simply end up with someone who is just a boss—nothing more and nothing less. In their mind they are there to manage other employees, keep the peace, and help the company stay afloat. If they can help make you into a better person and a better employee then that's great. If not, then that's okay because that's not their job anyway. Managing these bosses is not a very hard task. You can get them to help you by using the strategies given before combined with your own.

But then there are the *other* bosses. The bosses that spawned the creation of "managing your boss" books. The bosses that inspired movies like *Swimming With Sharks*. You have to see that movie. The bosses that help make psychiatrists rich, and occasionally push some employees to go postal. The *crazy* bosses. If you've never had to work for a boss you thought was hiding a mental illness then count your blessings because they're out there. The weird thing about crazy bosses though is that you can work for them for months without realizing who and what you're working with. They hardly ever strike you as odd during the interview. They may even appear normal during the first days and weeks on the job. But then you start to notice that your boss is a tad bit different from the ones you're used to. And then it dawns on you . . . my boss is crazy!

I've had my fair share of crazy bosses, and one or two of them made me question my own sanity. So what's a sane girl to do when faced with a boss that might have escaped from a psychiatric ward? Short of quitting your job or transferring to a different department, there's nothing much you can do but learn how to manage a crazy boss too. However, managing these bosses requires a different set of pointers. Read on for how to best recognize and manage each type of crazy boss.

The Bi-polar Boss

I know it sounds mean, but I had a boss that I just knew needed pills to help with a bi-polar disorder. He could be the most supportive and understanding boss on the planet, and then turn right around and tell me he wasn't going to help me with anything, that I was doing everything wrong, and that if I didn't like the way things were I could pick up my last paycheck because I was expendable. Sometimes I would cringe when the phone rang in anticipation of a verbal beat down.

Bi-polar bosses have mood swings that knock you over. They are prone to fits of rage that include cursing and threatening people. You never know whether they're going to promote you or fire you. In fact, they can do one right after the other. These bosses make you walk on eggshells because you can never guess how they are going to react to anything you or anyone else does. Even the simplest things like accidentally closing a door too hard can upset a bi-polar boss on the wrong day.

Management Tactics:
- *Stay out of their way:* If you can get away with a minimal amount of contact with them then do so.
- *Anticipate their mood swings:* After watching them do the Dr. Jekyll/Mr. Hyde transformation enough you may begin to see it coming. Get all you can out of them when they're feeling great, and be on your p's and q's when they're feeling foul.
- *Remind them of your worth:* Bi-polar bosses tend to forget how much they like you when they're in a bad mood. Gently remind them of their affinity towards you, stating how just the other day (or past hour) they were very pleased with you.
- *Develop a tough skin:* Learn to just deal with their personality, expecting some really great days and some stank ones.

The Obsessive-Compulsive Boss

A friend who worked for the same company I did, but had a different boss, once told me that she had a nightmare about answering the work phone on the third ring instead of on the second ring like she was supposed to, and her boss saw this and had an asthma attack. I could almost see it really happening; her boss was notorious for going berserk over lesser things. She started nearly every sentence with "Did you remember?" or "I hope you didn't." She also acted like her duty was to check everything my friend did for errors, which totally negated my friend's work since her job *was* checking for errors.

Always looking over your shoulder, the obsessive-compulsive boss thinks they're the only person that can do something right. On top of that they tend to be nitpicky, whiney and busybodies. These bosses act like they're your parents and they treat you like a toddler. What's worse, they expect everyone else to be as overanxious and anal as they are at work.

Management Tactics:
* *Help your boss trust you:* Point out all the great things you've done on your own. It may take a while, but once your boss sees that you can tie your shoes and handle projects without his or her assistance perhaps your boss will loosen up a little.
* *Become a little obsessive-compulsive yourself:* Make your boss feel like he or she isn't the only anal person in the office. Pay closer attention to the things your boss really cares about and talk to him or her about it. Seeing that you're concerned will relax his or her fears about you.

The Attention Deficit Disorder Boss

I had an ADD boss, and to this day I don't know how I worked with him without pulling out my hair. I felt like I was his mother after having to constantly remind him of things he said he would do. At other times I felt like his maid from doing things he should have been doing.

With an ADD boss you'll be unable to figure out what intelligent person hired him or her, much less promoted the person to a supervisory position. Besides having a blatant attention deficit disorder, ADD bosses just don't know what they're doing. You'll find them asking you for advice, missing deadlines, messing up projects, and goofing off on the job. This displeases you because there's stuff they're supposed to be teaching you, and you can't get your work done because you rely on them.

Management Tactics:
- *Make sure you're on the ball:* One day upper management is going to figure out what they hired and the ADD boss will be fired. You don't want them thinking you were playing around too. Make a list of all your accomplishments and/or document your work. Don't rely on the ADD boss to remember anything you did.
- *Make decisions for your boss:* ADD bosses tend to not like making decisions so attempt to make them for them. Tell them what you're going to do instead of asking like you normally would. If they disagree with your decision then they're forced to make one. This keeps you from waiting around for them to make up their mind.
- *Emphasize your deadlines:* ADD bosses have to be helped to remember everything from you asking for a specific day off to giving you information you need to complete a project. Emphasize every important deadline you give them and write it down somewhere for them to see.
- *Get help from someone else:* If you're supposed to be learning specific skills on the job and your boss isn't helping then go to someone else for assistance. Don't let ADD bosses keep you from growing on the job.

The Oppositional Defiance Disorder Boss

One of my old roommates had an ODD boss. Every other day she would come home saying how she was going to quit. Her boss called people bad names, yelled at employees, constantly threatened to fire people, and got upset about the weirdest things like her employees taking lunch breaks together or meeting each other after hours. She did not understand what "camaraderie" meant, and definitely did not promote it.

Grumpy and argumentative, these bosses walk around with a boulder on their shoulders 24/7. They argue for the sake of arguing, and will disagree with you about anything. When they find out you're right they don't apologize, they get even more ignorant. These bosses are unclear about everything, except that they're always right.

Management Tactics:
- *Avoid Disagreements:* Disagreeing with them is pointless. Don't even try. If they want to say they wrote the Bible then nod your head and keep working. If they ask you a question and you know there's a specific answer they want to hear then smile and give it to them.
- *Be Specific:* When you talk to them state what you have to say clearly and concisely. Leave no room for assumptions or questions. This way they will have a harder time twisting your words around, and won't have too much to say or ask afterward.

The Sadistic Boss

Kevin Spacey played this type of boss in *Swimming With Sharks*. My mother wanted me to watch the movie so I could see that my bi-polar boss wasn't so bad.

While the other bosses may get on your last nerves, this boss might actually scare you. In fact, it's suspected that the sadist boss isn't crazy at all. No, this type of boss may actually be evil. How else can you explain why they embarrass their subordinates in front of clients, demand employees to stick to deadlines superwoman couldn't meet, laugh as they disapprove raises without giving a reason, and assign super smart employees to the most menial of tasks? They like being mean and enjoy seeing people below them squirm. These are the bosses that cause employees to break down and cry, quit, then come back and shoot up the office. Working for sadistic bosses is hell at work.

Management Tactics:
- *Quit:* Quit before you get used to being treating like dirt, and let everyone else run over you too.
- *Quit:* Quit while you still have good self-esteem because a sadistic boss will strip you of it.
- *Quit:* Quit while you're still sane and don't need to see a psychiatrist.
- *Quit:* Quit before you start scheming on how to hurt your boss and end up in jail.
- *Quit:* Quit while you're still breathing because you don't know just how sadistic your boss really is.
- *Quit:* Quit before you're in the building when an ex-employee comes in wearing a black trench coat.

If you'll notice, confronting your crazy boss about his or her behavior was not one of the management tactics listed. This is because confrontation seldom works with crazy bosses. In a perfect world, you would be able to calmly and delicately explain that there are certain behaviors your boss exhibits that trouble you. And in that perfect world your boss would be appalled that he or she was perceived that way and would promise to make an effort to change. But this is the real world. It's likely that your boss' personality is as set in stone as yours. And no boss will probably like being told that you feel he or she is obsessive, childish, domineering, or ignorant—no matter how nice you put it. If you truly want to keep your position, your best bet is to change the way you act to fit what your boss believes is normal and appropriate. If you can't do that while working for a crazy boss, then do the sane thing and find another job.

Chapter 18

Handling Conflicts With Co-workers

*"Whenever you're in conflict with someone,
there is one factor that can make the difference between
damaging your relationship and deepening it.
That factor is attitude."*
—William James

I had barely been working two weeks at my first job after graduation when I found myself about to have an anxiety attack over a co-worker. You would think that getting along with her would be easy, considering we only had to interact via the phone and internet, but she has been the hardest person I've ever had to work with. Those simple interactions, which took place every day, left me upset and frustrated at least twice a week. I was serving as managing editor of a newspaper in Houston that had the layout done in an entirely different city, by her. She was used to putting the articles on any page she desired, and now I was supposed to tell her which should be the main stories and so on. Well, nearly every time I got the paper it looked nothing like I expected. To solve this, I eventually worked it out so that I could see the layout before it was printed and ask her to make adjustments. Beyond that problem, I felt that she tried to undermine my relationship with my boss, whom I seldom saw because he worked in the same office she did. Instead of calling me about any problems she saw caused by a story, such as one she was having a hard time laying out because of its length, she would complain to him about it and blow the problem out of proportion. He would in turn call me all perturbed, asking me about a problem I had never even heard about and thus hadn't been able to solve.

After talking with her about going straight to him with problems I could easily fix she stopped doing it—so much. I continued to have other problems with her, however, which I felt were mostly caused by a misunderstanding of job duties, her feeling like I took away some of her decision-making power, and a general personality conflict. Every time the phone rang I would pray it wasn't her. And we were always somewhat short with each other when we spoke—as if we both could not wait to hang up the phone. It got to the point that we stopped trying to hide our irritation with each other and became downright rude. When we didn't feel like being rude to each other, we would have other people relay our messages, which was childish and unproductive. While I did handle all the major work problems we had as they arose, I never took the time to go ahead and acknowledge and discuss the tension between us. Had I done so, perhaps work would have been less stressful for both of us.

Whether you have a cushy part-time job, an in by 9 a.m. out by 4:59 p.m. "gotta pay the bills" gig, or are climbing the corporate ladder in a grueling, yet satisfying salaried position, it's likely that you'll have a conflict with at least one co-worker at some point in time. Because of this, learning how to effectively handle conflicts with co-workers is very important.

Gone are the days when you really didn't care if you got fired and freely talked behind a co-worker's back, avoided them like an annoying ex-boyfriend, or even worse, straight cursed them out. You're not working to have some extra change to go to a step show or the movies anymore. You're working to pay all the bills and live the good life. You can't do this if you lose your job from being involved in a messy dispute at work. Bosses have no time to play referee, regardless of who started it. And you have no time to waste your time feuding with people on the job. Work can be hectic enough without the added pressure of mounting problems with your co-workers.

When you find yourself in difficult situations with co-workers, it may help you to reflect upon these very basic truths:

Your Co-Workers Aren't You: Sometimes we forget that we aren't the only one with an opinion. Other people may not see things exactly the way we do. What you find unacceptable and rude at work may not faze the next person. What you believe is a wonderful idea may be ridiculous to any number of people at your company. You can't expect your co-workers to think or act the way you do because they're operating from their own point of view. What you can do is learn to adapt to your co-workers' personalities, and try to understand where they are coming from in any given situation. By recognizing the differences you have with your co-workers (from your work styles to pet peeves), you'll be better able to work with them and handle conflicts when they arise.

Your Co-Workers Have Issues Just Like You: Your co-workers have issues just like you, and you never know what they're going through. They have money problems, relationship problems, self-esteem problems, health problems, and a multitude of other personal conundrums you'll never know about. They aren't going to be able to come to work everyday in their very best mood, just like you aren't.

Your Co-Workers Want To Be Liked Just Like You: As hard as it may be to believe sometimes, few of your co-workers ever intentionally do or say things to cause conflicts in the workplace.

Hardly any of them will ever "be out to get you," and most don't come to work to make your life or anyone else's miserable. They want to be liked and respected just like you. They don't want to be thought of as a backstabber, idiot, brown-noser or mean-spirited person. When a co-worker does or says something that upsets you, try giving them the benefit of the doubt that they didn't mean to, instead of assuming they said or did something on purpose. Thinking in this frame of mind will take you off of the defensive and allow you to better discuss the issues you feel should be addressed.

Pet Peeve or Real Problem?

The key to handling conflicts with co-workers is to attempt to make amends with the person you're having difficulties with as soon as you realize there's a "real problem." A real problem is one that keeps you from doing your job effectively or upsets your sense of well-being. Someone "rubbing you the wrong way" is not a real problem. You not liking the way someone talks, walks or dresses doesn't qualify as a real problem. A co-worker that has stolen your idea, one who has lied about you, or a constantly rude and domineering person is someone you may have a real problem with.

When faced with what you feel is a conflict at work, take time to calm yourself down and write down exactly what this person is doing or not doing that is driving you batty. This can help you determine if they've broken one of your quirky pet peeves or if they've really over stepped their boundaries.

Once you've decided that you do have a real problem with this person, get out that piece of paper that you wrote down their faults on and write down your own. Be honest with yourself. Have you done anything to provoke this person to act unfriendly towards you? Do you know they were talking behind your back because you were talking behind theirs and found out? Think long and think hard. The person may be reacting negatively to your negativity. But regardless of who started acting funny first, you should be the bigger person and end the drama.

Ending the Drama: Five Simple Steps

Step 1: Approach the person at the end of the work day or when you both have time to kill at work. Make sure no one is around to hear the conversation. If you are constantly around other people, politely and discreetly ask if you could please discuss something with them in private when they have time.

Step 2: Get to the point immediately by tactfully telling them what you want to discuss. Example: "I didn't want to interrupt you, but I feel that there is tension between us and I want us to be able to work in peace together." Or, "It seems there has been a misunderstanding between us and I want to clear it up so we can work comfortably around each other." However, when you begin the conversation keep in mind that your end goal is to have the issue resolved, not to put someone in his or her place. Never start the conversation with a rude question or statement. Example: "Do you have a problem with me?" Or by blaming the person for something. Example: "I know you've been talking behind my back." The person may have been wanting to clear up the problem as much as you. Approaching them in a negative manner will make the situation worse.

Step 3: Whether the person acknowledges that there's a problem ("Yes, I feel like there's tension between us too"), or plays dumb ("Girl, I call everyone a dumb bitch"), be specific about the problem and give examples while stating your case. Don't blame the person by telling them what they have done to you. Tell them that you are offended because it "seems like," or "appears" or you "feel like" something has happened.
Right: "For the past two weeks I've felt like you've purposefully belittled me in front of our manager. Last Monday you told our manager that the last marketing assistant caught on much quicker than I did, and just yesterday I heard you whisper to her that 'it would probably take too much of her time to teach me our new software, from the looks of how slow I've been on

other jobs.'"

Wrong: "I don't know if you're trying to make yourself look smart in front of the boss by talking bad about me all day long, but it's getting on my nerves."

Right: "When I first started working here we seemed to get along great, but for the past two weeks it seems like you've been giving me the cold shoulder by ignoring my questions, or cutting me off when I'm talking to you."

Wrong: "You've been acting funny towards me for a long time and I know I haven't done anything to you."

Step 4: Give the person time to respond to what you've said. It's likely that your co-worker will acknowledge that there is a problem, but the reason for it may be far different from what you were thinking. As stated before, they may feel that they were just reacting to an offense you committed against them. On the flip side, they may deny that a problem even exists. If so, at least they will be more conscious of how they interact with you. Regardless of what they say, take care to watch your body language and tone of voice.

Step 5: If they acknowledge that an issue does need to be cleared up, be sincere when you tell them that you would like to work out the problem. Attempt to come up with a solution that you both feel is appropriate.

Here's how Carla handled two conflicts she encountered:

Carla's First Confrontation:

Carla is a 23-year-old writer for her city's alternative newspaper. She has what she feels is a major issue with one of her editors, Rick. She feels that Rick, who happens to be white, over edits her articles when they focus on African-Americans. She has had this problem with Rick for about five months, but she just got up the nerve to say something about it. She understands her need to maintain a good working relationship with Rick, so she's intent on confronting him in a mature way that will get the issue resolved.

Carla: "Hello Rick. I was hoping I could talk to you about something before the day is over."

Rick: "What's on your mind Keshia?"

Carla: "It's Carla, not Keshia, Rick."

Rick: "Oh, I'm sorry. What's wrong Carla?"

Carla: "Well, I want you to know that I think you're doing a great job as the art and entertainment editor, but sometimes it seems like you're a little biased when editing my articles."

Rick: "How's that?"

Carla: "Well, every time I've written an article covering an African-American group or event, you've cut my story almost in half without giving me an explanation, and you've changed certain words I used like 'phat' to 'awesome.' I also feel that you've questioned my judgment at times, without a good reason. For example, last month you changed the rating I gave Outkast's new CD from five stars to three."

Rick: "I had legitimate reasons to make all of those changes. No one uses the word 'phat,' and I'm sure that Outkast's CD wasn't that 'tight,' as you like to say."

Carla: "Rick, I have to be honest and tell you that I don't understand your reasoning. Just because you don't use that word doesn't mean my readers don't or that they don't understand the lingo. And how would you know the CD wasn't worth five stars if you haven't listened to it?"

Rick: "Well, my black friend Kevin said he would give the CD three stars if he had to rate it."

Carla: "Rick, I was told by the managing editor that the ratings are up to me. And when you change my words like that you change my style and voice. Could you please also explain to me why you cut my articles in half?"

Rick: "I just thought our readers wouldn't be that interested in things like a black holocaust exhibit."

Carla: "Did you see how many emails and letters I got thanking me for 'showcasing an enlightening and heart wrenching exhibit that all Americans should see?'"

Rick: "I can't say that I did."

Carla: "Rick, I was hoping it was just a coincidence that you shorten my articles focusing on African-Americans. I can understand that we may have two different perspectives on which stories are important, but I don't feel it's right of you to shorten my articles the way you do. You wrote a three-page article on Elvis Presley last week, who's dead, and just last month you ran Susan's five-page article on the Jewish holocaust. How do you think that makes me feel, and what do you think that makes me think about you?"

Rick: "I can see your point. I'm not prejudiced, but maybe I was a little bit biased. What do you want me to do?"

Carla: "I would like for you to discuss major changes you

	want to make with me before you submit my article to run—as you did with all other writers."
Rick:	"Sometimes I don't have time for that."
Carla:	"I can understand that. During those times I'm sure I won't have a problem getting the managing editor to let someone else edit my documents due to your schedule."
Rick:	"That won't be necessary. We can go over the story you're currently working on today and hopefully we can start getting this little glitch worked out."
Carla:	"Thank you so much Rick."

It looks like Carla may have to work a little bit with Rick, but she definitely got her point across in an intelligent and mature manner. She may never want to hang out with Rick after hours, but at least he is going to make an effort to stop "over editing" her stories.

Carla's Second Confrontation:

Carla is holding down a second job as a marketing assistant for a large marketing agency. She has a conflict with one of her co-workers, Tory, that has been brewing since she started working there a month ago. She's not sure why, but Tory just doesn't seem to like her, as her rude and hurtful comments indicate. She has to work closely with Tory, an African-American female who is also 23, so she's decided to talk to Tory about the conflict they seem to have.

Carla:	"Excuse me Tory, would it be possible for us to discuss something during our lunch break?"
Tory:	"Like what?"
Carla:	"Well, I feel like there is tension between us and I'd like to talk about it."

Tory: "We can talk now."

Carla: "I'm unsure if I've done anything to offend you, but sometimes it seems like you are trying to belittle me in front of our manager. For example, last Monday you told our manager that the last marketing assistant caught on much quicker than I did, and just yesterday I heard you whisper to her that it would probably take too much of her time to teach me our new software, from the looks of how slow I've been on other jobs."

Tory: "Well, when you first started working here you acted like no one could tell you anything and like you were smarter than everyone else."

Carla: "Really? When?"

Tory: "I can't pinpoint all the times, but it got on my nerves. And the only reason I said that to the manager was because you acted like you knew everything in front of her, but asked other employees a lot of questions when she wasn't around."

Carla: "I'm sorry if I came off that way to you. That's not how I feel or how I want to be perceived. This is my first real job out of college and I'm trying to do my best. Still, I wish you would have told me how you felt instead of saying those negative things to the manager."

Tory: "Well, that was wrong of me. I apologize."

Carla: "Well, it's cool. I'm glad that's behind us. I hope that we can get along better now."

Tory: "I hope so too."

Maybe Carla was acting a bit snotty, maybe not. At least she tactfully confronted Tory before the tension built up further. Those scenarios were played out in a win-win fashion, but not all confrontations go that smoothly. What is Carla supposed to do if her confrontations are played out like this?:

Carla's First Confrontation Revisited:

Carla: "Good morning Rick. I was hoping I could talk to you about something before the day is over."

Rick: "I'm very busy Keshia, but I guess I can give you a minute."

Carla: "It's Carla, not Keshia, Rick."

Rick: "Oh. You two just look so much alike. What's the problem Carla?"

Carla: "Well, I want you to know that I think you're doing a great job as the art and entertainment editor, but sometimes it seems like you're a little biased when editing my articles."

Rick: "I'm an excellent editor, and I'm not biased in any way."

Carla: "Well, perhaps you're not, but I've noticed some things. Every time I've written an article covering an African-American group or event you've cut my story almost in half without giving me an explanation, and you've changed certain words I used like "phat" to "awesome." I also feel that you've questioned my judgment at times, without a good reason. For example, last month you changed the rating I gave Outkast's new CD from five stars to three."

Rick: "Educated people don't use the word 'phat,' and my black friend Kevin said that Outkast's CD wasn't that 'tight,' as you like to say."

Carla: "I have undergraduate degrees in marketing and journalism from Columbia and am working on my master's in African-American studies. I am educated and use the word 'phat' all the time, Rick. And I was told by the managing editor that the ratings are up to me."

Rick: "Well, I've never seen anyone write that word or other slang terms you use, and you have to remember that you're not just writing for a black audience."

Carla: "But I'm not writing for just a white one either, and when you change my words like that you change my style and voice. Will you please explain why you cut my articles in half?"

Rick: "I just thought our readers wouldn't be that interested in things like a reparations debate or a black holocaust exhibit. Writing about things like that just makes tension run deeper between black and white Americans, and it over exaggerates the trials black people experienced during slavery. I never read about anything like that in college."

Carla: "I didn't read about that kind of stuff in college either, probably because someone didn't consider it worth including in the history books. Educating black and white readers about black history is important to me, Rick. Did you see how many emails and letters I got

	thanking me for 'showcasing an enlightening and heart wrenching exhibit that all Americans should see?'"
Rick:	"No, but Kevin said most black people want to forget about slavery and aren't interested in reparations."
Carla:	"Rick, I was hoping it was just a coincidence that you shorten my articles focusing on African-Americans. I can understand that we may have two different perspectives on which stories are important, but I don't feel it's right of you to shorten my articles the way you do. You wrote a three-page article on Elvis Presley last week, who's dead, and just last month you ran Susan's five-page article on the Jewish holocaust. How do you think that makes me feel, and what do you think that makes me think about you?"
Rick:	"Look Keshia . . . maybe you would be better off working at a minority-owned newspaper or magazine. I think you're way too ethnocentric. I stand behind my editorial changes and I'll cut in half what I want to cut in half, and I'll run what I choose to run."
Carla:	"My name is Carla, Rick. And I wish you didn't feel that way, but I will make it a point to discuss this issue with the managing editor today."
Rick:	"That's fine. If we're through I've got stories to edit."

Carla's Second Confrontation Revisited:

Carla: "Excuse me Tory, would it be possible for us to discuss something during our lunch break?"

Tory: "What is it?"

Carla: "Well, I feel like there is tension between us and I'd like to talk about it."

Tory: "You're damn right there's tension and it's not my fault."

Carla: "Excuse me? I'm unsure if I've done anything to offend you, but sometimes it seems like you are trying to belittle me in front of our manager. For example, last Monday you told our manager that the last marketing assistant caught on much quicker than I did, and just yesterday—."

Tory: "I never said that."

Carla: "I was right there when you said that and everyone else heard it too."

Tory: "Well, maybe I did, but it's only because you act like your shit don't stink and like you're so smart and pretty. The only reason you got this job is because my friend quit."

Carla: "What do you mean, 'like my shit don't stink'?"

Tory: "You acted like you were ready to run the company when you first stepped in, and you brown-nosed the manager. I guess you think you're better than everyone else because you got a new Acura, natural hair, and your man is half-way cute."

Carla: "I'm sorry if I came off that way to you, that's certainly not how I want to be perceived. This is my first real job out of college and I'm trying to do my best. Still, I wish you would have told me how you felt instead of saying those negative things to the manager."

Tory: "Oh well, I wouldn't have said those things if you didn't act so prissy. Is that all you wanted to talk about? I'm busy."

There's not much of a chance that Carla will want to be in the same room with Tory or Rick after those incidents. Reasoning with both of these rude and arrogant people didn't work. Carla may have to have a small talk with her manager if Tory continues acting ignorant, and she will definitely need to discuss Rick's attitude and perception with the managing editor as soon as possible. Sometimes all you can do is try. When it appears that your co-worker just doesn't want to act right there are still other ways to end the drama.

When All Else Fails

Involve Your Supervisor: It may temporarily create more tension, but getting someone with some authority to handle the conflict may be the only way to stop the madness. You should approach your supervisor about the conflict and just lay it out plainly and calmly. Explain how you tried and failed to resolve the issue on your own, and how you really want this conflict resolved as soon as possible. This way you'll cover your butt (in case the other person talked to your supervisor first) and you'll be closer to working in peace.

Steer Clear Of Your Co-Worker: If you can work in a different team, room or office without inconveniencing yourself, then it may be wise to do so. Don't view this as running away—you're saving yourself from more drama.

Regardless of what happens in situations with your co-workers, you have to stay cool. Never allow anyone to turn you into a yelling, cursing, crying or fighting person on the job. You'll disgrace yourself in front of your boss and fellow co-workers, even if everyone knows you're not the one with the problem. Remember that part of working in a professional position means being a professional.

Chapter 19

Working Around Office Politics

"As far as possible, without surrender, be on good terms with all persons."
—Max Ehrmann

I found out a long time ago that the word "grown up" simply refers to someone who can be considered an adult, not necessarily a mature or professional person. If you haven't discovered it yet, this fact is apparent at most companies.

When I was a teenager changing minimum-wage jobs frequently, and even when I took my first semi-professional position as an editorial assistant, I learned that so-called grown ups could be just as immature, irrational and simple-minded as the children they were raising. However, unlike their kids they can also be vindictive and messy, especially when they are given a little power at work.

It is nearly inevitable that you will work in an environment that will remind you of your old college yard. You'll quickly notice that certain people don't like each other and entire groups of people seem pitted against one another. And somehow, at some point in time, you'll feel as if you're in the middle of them. One of your co-workers will pull you aside to tell you to "watch out for so and so" and how horrible a person he or she is. People in a team or department you are working in will bad-mouth and attempt to sabotage another group they feel aren't doing their jobs effectively. Your boss might even whisper that you should avoid a couple of people he or she happens to loathe, and promise you one of their jobs.

Of course you want to avoid being sucked into all of the drama some of your colleagues seem to thrive off of. You find the secrecy, back-stabbing and unprofessional behavior they exhibit to be appalling. But it is hard to stay out of office politics because you work closely and depend on so many of these people. So, short of jumping into all of the ongoing frays, what do you do? More importantly, what do you *not* do? I've found that you can't avoid office politics, but you can work around it.

How to Work Around Office Politics

Observe your environment: Take careful mental notes of who doesn't like who, and why, through the unasked for stories your co-workers will tell you. Don't ask any of them to elaborate, just listen. Consider it a form of entertainment.

Avoid making decisions about your colleagues based on other people's judgments: You should already have learned that you can't believe everything you hear—this is especially true in the workplace. People will have motives for telling you certain things about others, and you'll probably find that most of what you're told are half-truths or outright lies. You can listen to other people's warnings, but reserve your judgment. It would be a shame for you to dodge interacting with a potentially fantastic co-worker because of someone else's opinion.

Avoid giving your personal opinion about the conflicts taking place at your company: If you find that you can trust one or two of your colleagues then you can share your thoughts about all the drama going on. However, stay away from "water-cooler" type conversations or giving your take on a situation to a random co-worker. Otherwise your feedback may be a part of the next water-cooler meeting.

Avoid showing the appearance of taking sides: You are likely to feel that someone is in the wrong in certain situations; however, unless you are directly involved in it you shouldn't deliberately show whose side you are on. Don't write any letters stating your views on a personal work dispute, don't talk to your boss about your views, and don't tell the co-worker you feel is behaving badly that you think he or she is wrong. When you show that you are on one person's side it automatically puts you on other people's bad sides, and you may not even know it.

Avoid playing the mediator: Unless you work in the HR department as a mediator you shouldn't attempt to help co-workers solve work disputes. You should even stay out of conflicts between people you consider good friends who don't get along. Once you put yourself in the middle of them you will find yourself taking sides.

Try to minimize your interaction with blatantly messy or troublesome colleagues: Becoming friends with co-workers who are constantly involved in office politics will reflect badly upon you and create automatic enemies. Avoid people who seem to strategize about how to make others look bad, or who use their influence to get people in trouble. Once you accidentally piss off these types of people they may devise schemes to ruin your reputation also. And of course you won't have anyone to turn to because befriending them made you the second most hated person at work.

Chapter 20

Working in Corporate America: Sink or Swim?

*"America, be placed on notice. We know who we are.
We understand our collective power.
Following today we will act on that power."*
—Maxine Waters

The term "corporate America" means different things to different people. To some individuals corporate America creates thoughts of multinational corporations housed in sky-high buildings with more employees than can be counted. Others define corporate America by the environment it often fosters: competitive, impersonal and mercenary. Yet to the large majority of African-Americans the term corporate America brings to mind these pictures and more. The truth is that when many of us envision corporate America, we picture a work environment that's dominated by white people. And we think of it as a somewhat unwelcoming place—a place that has traditionally been harder for us to enter than whites, and harder for us to succeed in.

Nevertheless, as a larger number of companies have begun to embrace diversity, more African-Americans have gravitated towards working in a corporate environment. Working for big businesses can provide more money, more prestige, and more opportunities to have a greater effect in one's chosen industry than working for smaller and less recognized companies. However, despite the positives, there are still aspects of working in corporate America that people of color may find disheartening. The following are issues African-Americans tend to have while working in a corporate environment.

Issue 1—It's a Lonely Place For African-Americans
If you went to a predominantly white college you'll have more of an idea of what working in corporate America feels like than those who attended HBCUs. In 2005, African-Americans made up just 8.1 percent of the management and professional workforce, so just like you'll always find more white than black people at most colleges so will you in corporate America. You may feel very uncomfortable when you walk into a room of a dozen or more people and realize you're the only black person there. And when you finally realize that there's not a single black face in the entire building besides yours, you may start to feel very lonely and out of place.

Issue 2—African-Americans Receive Little Recognition
The thought that African-Americans have to work twice as hard as their white counterparts to be recognized and rewarded for their hard work is considered true in most working environments, but it is considered a fact of life by African-Americans working in corporate America. Many African-Americans also feel that despite their education, having earned a position in the company and doing well there, they still have to continually prove that they belong in corporate America. Unlike their white counterparts, whose work is allowed to speak for itself, African-Americans may find that their intellect and ability to perform is always under question, as if affirmative action or a bad hiring

decision is what landed them the job. Beyond this, African-Americans may find that they are slower to get promoted than their white counterparts, slower to get raises, and slower to get work or projects that actually utilize their skills and abilities.

Issue 3 —It Doesn't Embrace Cultural Differences
Because corporate America is largely controlled by white males, they define what is acceptable regarding everything from speech, to dress, to hair styles. Some can appreciate cultural expression, but others feel that if they don't speak it, if they don't wear it, and if they can't comb it that way then you shouldn't either. And when they don't know if something is appropriate, they may look at white women to find out.

Issue 4 —It's Too Competitive
Everyone is trying to climb the corporate ladder at the same time, and some people will pull you down to beat you to the top. This can create excess stress among employees who feel like they always have to be ahead of the next person. It's difficult to have camaraderie among employees in an environment that's so divisive. Beyond this, some companies may pit blacks against other blacks as they vie for positions earmarked (openly or discreetly) to minorities.

Issue 5—It Can Be Grueling
Don't expect to work 9-5 everyday in corporate America. You'll be lucky if you don't take work home. Projects come first, not drinks after work, exercise or beauty rest. The long hours can interfere with people's family and social lives.

Issue 6—It's Unstable
Because corporate America is so money driven, owners always do what they must to cut costs or make a profit. This can equate to thousands of layoffs at a time in large corporations. It's difficult to work well and enjoy your work when everyone knows you may not have a job unless so much money is earned in a certain

quarter, or your company is about to be bought out, again.

Catalyst, a leading research and advisory organization working to advance women in business, revealed in their 2005 report titled "2005 Catalyst Census of Corporate Officers and Top Earners of the Fortune 500," that African-American women represented only 1.1 percent of corporate officers in the 260 Fortune 500 companies they surveyed that verified race/ethnicity and gender data. African-American men held 2.6 percent of all corporate officer positions.

Catalyst's 2004 report titled "Advancing African-American Women in the Workplace: What Managers Need to Know," discussed the barriers African-American women said they faced in the professional workplace. The barriers included negative, race-based stereotypes, more frequent questioning of their credibility and authority, and a lack of institutional support. According to the report, African-American women also reported experiencing a "double outsider" status—unlike white women or African-American men who share gender or race in common with most colleagues or managers—and conflicting relationships with white women.

As a black woman you can't afford to be oblivious to the fact that corporate America's environment basically works against you, not for you. This doesn't mean you can't climb the corporate ladder, shatter the glass ceilings you may face, and do as well or better than your white counterparts. You can do this and more. You're just going to have to be prepared for anything as you work your way up.

Swimming in the Corporate Environment

1. Have a Plan: If your goal is to climb the corporate ladder at the company you're working for then you'll need to know how to climb it. It may not be a typical straight ladder—parts of it might be broken off and it may zig-zag. So have a plan before you start climbing. You'll first need to know what rung on the ladder you're starting from and how many steps you need to climb to get to where you want to be. Find out what the people in the positions you desire did to get to where they are. Where did they start on the ladder? How many years did it take them to get the position they have? How many times did they get promoted? What was special about them? What advice can they give you? Knowing these things will help you map out a plan to get you to the rung on the ladder you desire.

2. Adapt To a Predominantly White Environment: You must be able to act comfortable around your non-black co-workers. Because they control the environment you also have to ensure that they feel comfortable around you if you want to succeed. For the most part, this can be done by being the professional you should be. However, making some white people more comfortable with you may take any number of actions, which might include not talking about "black issues" on the job to not wearing your hair in natural styles. Sadly, the less "black" you act or look often makes whites more accepting of you. This is not to say that you have to or should change anything about yourself. I personally won't work for a company that makes me hesitant to say the word "black" aloud, or makes me feel the need to press my hair or not wear ethnic clothing. Whether you choose to conform on the job is a personal choice.

3. Gather Support: Feelings of alienation on the job can lead to a lot of stress and possibly make you perform poorly. And no one wants to spend eight hours of their day feeling vulnerable and lonesome. But chances are that your situation isn't half as bad as you think. Feelings of alienation are strengthened when you assume that your non-black co-workers and employers will be less friendly and supportive of you because of your ethnicity. Most intelligent people realize that you don't have to share someone's skin color to work well with them and develop friendships. However, when working in a predominantly white environment you may have to be the one that reaches out to your co-workers for support, and that's okay. If you don't find enough support on the job then you'll have to get it after hours. Build up a support group of other professionals, family and friends that reinforce your sense of adequacy and make you feel more secure about your position at work as a black woman.

4. Get a Career Mentor: Having a career mentor, someone that is dedicated to helping you in your career, is critical to your success. Though you can have a mentor outside your company, if you work in a corporate environment you definitely need someone who works with you. Seek out someone with influence that appears sincere and amiable when talking to you. They can serve as a mentor in an unofficial capacity or you can actually ask them to be your mentor.

5. Be Better Than the Best: Just "doing your job" in an atmosphere filled with competitive people isn't going to get you one step up the corporate ladder. You have to show your employer that you can do more than hang with the big boys; they shouldn't have anything on you. Make yourself the employee that other employees come to for help, and if possible, who your manager comes to for advice sometimes. If you're better than the best, then when the time comes for a promotion there shouldn't be one reason why your boss doesn't consider you first.

6. Learn to Speak Up for Yourself: Do not ignore signs of discrimination. Your talent and energy helps keep the company in business. Speak up if you find you're being treated differently than other co-workers. Speak up if you feel excluded; speak up if you feel other people's biases are affecting you. Don't let anyone get the impression that you can be ignored, taken for granted, and not considered a valuable employee that deserves the same opportunities and respect as everyone else.

7. Develop a Tough Skin: Working in corporate America may send you home crying some days if you don't develop a tough skin soon after you enter it. The environment isn't fit for people who can't stand pressure in many forms—black or white. You'll need to be tougher and more flexible when you walk into work everyday. And you have to adopt the attitude that you're going to excel in the corporate environment regardless of any barriers set before you.

Chapter 21

Networking Effectively

"Each person represents a world in us, a world possibly not born until they arrive, and it is only by this meeting that a new world is born in us."
—Anais Nin

Shyness is not one of my attributes. I've learned to ask for what I want—as nicely as possible—from those who have the power to give it to me. I've found that if you're sincere in your desires and approach people correctly, most people are more than willing to help you. Sometimes, though, finding people to help you is much harder than actually getting them to help you.

After I decided to uproot myself from Texas to New York to pursue a career in book publishing, one of the first things I did was seek out people in the field who could give me advice and job leads. I was taken out to breakfast by the owner of a very influential media website after I expressed my love of her website and future goal of entrepreneurship. Because I was taking publishing classes I had access to many publishing executives who came to speak to my class. I hardly ever missed a chance to talk with them after class and to get their email address so I could tell them about my interests. I also went to seminars, conferences, and even book signings that I knew publishing professionals might attend. My networking led to freelance work, actual jobs and new friends.

Yet some people cringe when they hear the word "networking," especially those just starting out in their careers. The idea of "meeting and greeting" strangers intimidates them, and seeking out people who can possibly help them advance professionally brings out the fear of rejection. Yet, the old adage, "It's not what you know, but who you know," could not be truer for African-American women. Our social/business circles tend to contain mainly other African-Americans, and given the racial makeup of American businesses and those who hire for them this isn't very beneficial. In other words: black people aren't the only group you should be networking with!

Networking is what the most successful and savviest business professionals say got them to where they are today. They built mutually beneficial relationships that served as a support system and boosted their careers. Building up a network of people that will help you grow and thrive is a task you'll be both consciously and unconsciously doing for the rest of your life. You have to always be on the lookout for people in both high and low places that can be added to your network. There are individuals out there who can help you land your dream job, turn you on to professions you never thought twice about, give you an idea to bring in truckloads of dough, or simply change your life just by being supportive—and you haven't even met them yet. And you won't if you don't make networking an ongoing task. There are various ways you can build your network:

- Through colleagues and business associates.
- Through memberships in professional and civic organizations.
- Through your relatives, friends, and their peers.
- Through religious involvement.
- Through social functions and community events.
- Through volunteering.

♦ Through conferences for people in your profession.

Most of the networking you'll do will take place informally—with people you'll meet without even trying. But there will likely be a host of events organized for the sole purpose of networking that you will attend. Walking into one of these events alone may bring back the same butterflies you felt on the first day of school when you were looking for a place to sit at lunch. While it may have seemed like you were the only lonely looking girl struggling to find a seat next to someone cool, the majority of the girls probably felt the same way, and maybe were hoping you'd sit by them so they wouldn't look so lonely.

That's just how networking events are. No one wants to look lonely, unimportant and bored. Everyone came to mix and mingle, and chances are that if you approach someone they'll be relieved that you did. The following are networking tips for you to utilize.

Before the Function:
♦ Review your purpose for attending the function. Are you coming to meet a specific person, get some contacts in your profession, or just learn more about the hosts of the function?
♦ Plan to arrive on time for the function. If you're attending a meeting that offers networking before it starts, arrive early enough to participate in the networking portion of the meeting.
♦ Create a 20-30 second introduction about yourself. Example: "Hi! I'm Shiloh Davis. I'm a graduate student in sociology at Texas Southern University and I plan on becoming a sociology professor. Right now I'm searching for a position in the social service field to help finance my studies."
♦ Brainstorm a couple of questions that could help you get a conversation started.
♦ Have more than enough professional looking business cards with you, and make sure you have easy access to them.
♦ Make sure you are dressed appropriately. Professional networking events normally call for business casual attire.

At the Function:
- Greet people you know so you can be introduced to others.
- Introduce yourself to the host of the event. Request introductions to people whom the host recommends you meet.
- Take the initiative to introduce yourself to other people, especially people who may have seen you once or twice but were never introduced to you.
- Introduce others to people you've just met.
- Exchange cards with the people you meet.

After the Function:
- Write a note to yourself on the back of the business cards you're given—something that will help jog your memory about people when you look at their cards again. Also include the date and name of the function.
- Contact those individuals who interested you, seeing how you may be able to help each other in some endeavor.
- Think about how you could have networked better. Did you miss out on an opportunity to meet someone because you were scared or didn't know how to break into a conversation? Did you neglect to tell people something important about you and your line of work? You did bring enough business cards, didn't you?

Becoming a networking pro may take a little time, but after enough of these events you'll be able to work a room of professionals like you worked a room full of your college peers at the parties you miss. The only difference is that working the room now could mean working your way up in your professional career.

Chapter 22

Losing Your Job Without Losing Yourself

"Every exit is an entry somewhere else."
—Tom Stoppard

The first job I was ever "relieved" from was as a concession stand clerk at a $1 dollar movie theater. I was 14 and technically was not old enough to have the job. But that's not why I got fired. I was let go for eating a hot dog. I was closing with my co-workers and we were supposed to throw the left over hot dogs away; we were forbidden to eat them. Back then I couldn't stand to abide by rules that didn't make sense to me, so, at my co-workers' urging (who said they wouldn't tell) I ate one. Of course, the same co-worker who said she ate them all the time told the manager the next day and I was fired as soon as I got to work. I was stunned about losing my job over a piece of meat and bread, but not really upset. After all, I didn't really have to work, and I wasn't supposed to be working anyway. I went home and enjoyed the rest of my day.

Eight years and probably a half dozen jobs later I was fired again. Yet this time I nearly wrecked my car as I went home because I couldn't see through my tears.

I was fired for asking my boss, publisher of the newspaper I edited, for money to pay for a root canal. I know it sounds weird, but it's true. My former boss, however, has always insisted that I quit, and I think he honestly believes this. So, to be fair, I'll just say that I got fired/quit, though the story behind why this happened still sounds farfetched and we don't agree on that either.

After going to the dentist I discovered that I needed not one, but two root canals, and very soon or else both teeth would need to be pulled. Now, why I let it get that bad is another story, but two root canals is what I needed.

After contemplating how I was going to pay for two root canals totaling about $1,000, I decided that I should ask my boss for the money. Here was my rationale: I did not have health insurance; it seemed like I was due a raise (which I was sure my boss couldn't afford, but I thought he might be able to afford two root canals); and I had just been nominated for a very prestigious national writing award. After convincing myself that my logic was sound, asking him to pay for two root canals, or even one, didn't seem like such a big deal. I couldn't have been more wrong.

One day my boss called from the sister office in a different city. He sounded all chipper, which everyone knew could change at any moment, so I decided to ask him while he was in a good mood. After explaining how my teeth ached and how I needed a root canal (I had decided to ask for just one initially), I asked him for the money as sweetly as I possibly could. Well, he laughed at me and then asked what made me think he should pay for my root canal with his money. I looked at the phone kind of funny when he said that because I couldn't tell whether he was being serious or playful. My boss was known for helping employees out with personal things, from paying their rent to getting a car (the former he had done for me). So, I decided he was being playful.

After explaining my rationale to him he became very quiet. Then he asked how much of a raise I wanted. I told him I was asking for money for a root canal and not a raise, at which point he just asked me again about the raise. I let out a sigh and decided to play along just in case he really was considering giving me a raise. Before we hung up, he said he'd talk to his wife, co-owner of the newspaper, about it and call me back.

Early the next morning he called me at the office and he didn't sound upbeat like the day before. He sounded pissed, and I knew that when he sounded like that I wasn't going to have a very good workday. He started half-yelling at me about how he couldn't believe I had the audacity to ask for a raise when he was already paying me more than he should. I felt nauseous. Was I losing my mind, or had I just asked him for a root canal? I tried to explain that I had never asked for a raise, but he told me that he knew what I had said. At that point I knew there was no point in arguing.

I unfolded the latest newspaper onto my desk like he asked me to and began going through it page by page as he told me what a bad job I was doing and why. Now I was nauseous and speechless. Less than two weeks ago he had been bragging on me to all of his colleagues about how good I was and how I was nominated for this special award, which he flew me to another state to receive in case I won. And now I wasn't even worth the money he gave me?

After berating me for a few more minutes he said he'd have to think about whether he wanted to even keep me now, and then he hung up the phone. I stared at my computer and started crying. I didn't know what was going on.

Later that day the newspaper's co-manager told me my boss had called him the night before sounding all upset and saying that I had demanded a raise. The co-manager said he was probably just having a lot of money problems right now, and that me just saying the word "money" had set him off. My boss called a couple of more times that day to talk to the co-manager about me and the "raise I demanded." He didn't want to talk to me at all, so I sat by helplessly as he went on and on about my lousy work and how he couldn't afford to give me a raise, much less the salary I was already receiving. Not wanting to get himself snapped at, the co-manager didn't do anything but listen as he went on with his verbal rampage.

When the last phone call from him came in I was exhausted from worrying and wondering how this had happened and why. My boss had gone left field on various people, but I never dreamed that he'd be like that towards me. The co-manager told me he was pretty sure my boss was going to let me go, and he asked me what I wanted to do. I told him that I really couldn't see myself working there anymore after the unprofessional way I had been treated. However, if he decided to let me go I would like to at least work another 30 days while I figured out what I was going to do with myself.

Still, when I left work I expected my boss to call me on my cell phone and talk the matter out with me. Or, I expected his wife, who had been like an adopted mother to me, to call me and ask what was going on. But I got a call from neither of them. The next morning the co-manager came into my office, sat in a chair with my last check in his lap looking all sad, and told me that my boss wanted me to pack my things and leave immediately. He had told him what I said about not being sure I wanted to work there anymore, and about asking for 30 more days if he decided to let me go, which I had not expected him to tell my boss. I was angry at the co-manager, who I thought could have done or said more to save my job. I was also dumfounded, and so was the rest of the staff. They thought it was a joke at first.

After the initial shock wore off, depression set in. A man who had given me my first real job out of college, and whom I had known and worked for since my senior year in high school, had just had someone else tell me I was fired. This was a man who I also loved and respected and who I thought loved and respected me. And to top it off, his wife, who I just knew would straighten things out, didn't call me or return my phone calls. I just didn't get it. And even though I have since made amends with both of them, and found out the situation was just as confusing and frustrating to them, I still can't figure out how that whole ordeal ever happened.

As you can tell by my story, getting fired or laid off can be a very traumatic experience. The ordeal is hard to shake off for individuals starting out in their careers, and those who have been working their way up in their chosen profession. Psychologists acknowledge that losing a job can cause as much stress as losing a loved one, and it's easy to see why. One of the first questions a stranger usually asks a person is what line of work he or she is involved in, thus it's no surprise that many people define themselves by their occupation. Jobs provide more than just a steady paycheck. Along with the money comes a sense of belonging, security and pride. Those special intangibles can be lost in a matter of moments. The added financial stress that job loss puts people through only makes matters worse. But despite this, you can't lose yourself to job loss. People from all walks of life have taken this bullet, survived, and been better off because of the experience—you can too. The following are suggestions for dealing with job loss and getting your career back on track.

Look Ahead

The best way for you to bounce back is to look ahead. You lost your job, but while doing so you have gained a chance to seek other opportunities—opportunities you never would have known existed had you not lost your job. So resist the urge to feel sorry for yourself, dwell on whatever you've lost, or be angry with the company or your former boss for the situation you're in. You have to concentrate on making a comeback and you can't do this if you're filled with regret, anger or sadness. Remember that the only person that can turn your career around is you. And the only person standing in your way of success is you. Once you've surveyed what you've lost, discover what you have to gain. Make the decision to make your job loss one of the best things that ever happened to your career.

I felt like a failure and as if the world was coming to an end when I was let go. But as I was surfing my computer for jobs a week later a thought popped into my mind from out of nowhere: You always wanted to get into book publishing; why don't you pursue a career in that? Hmmm, I thought, as I remembered how in college I wanted to edit books. That's not a bad idea.

That random thought of actually pursuing a career in book publishing, which I eventually did, would never have entered my mind or been taken seriously if I had been at work editing news articles that day, and not unemployed and miserable at home.

Focus On Your Finances

Unemployment takes many people by surprise as they realize that they aren't prepared to go without a steady paycheck. Count yourself blessed if you have money in the bank to pay your bills for a couple of months. If you don't, you're going to need to do a little maneuvering, especially if you are living on your own. Chances are you'll have to seriously scramble to pay your bills for a while. You may have to borrow money from your relatives or a bank until you can get yourself back on your feet. Do what you have to, but try to avoid taking on credit card debt. Find out if you are eligible to collect unemployment compensation and if so file for it immediately. You also have to cut back on spending immediately, even if you have money saved up. Now is not the time to go shopping excessively, go out to eat all the time, or spend large amounts of your cash on any form of entertainment.

I had been promising myself to save up for a rainy day since I got my first post-college paycheck. When the rainy day finally came in the form of job loss I had less than $1,000 in the bank and I needed some of that to pay bills. Likewise, a friend of mine who lost his job right after me had recently purchased a new car and signed a new apartment lease. We were so unlucky it was almost funny. He ended up having to break his lease and share an apartment with a friend, and I had to break my lease too and move home to claim my old bedroom. Although we eventually made it out of "brokenness," we both vowed never to be stuck in that kind of predicament again.

Be Patient

I know it's hard to be told to be patient when you're deciding how to spend your last twenty dollar bill, but impatience just adds to the stress. It takes most people months to find a job close to the one they had, or one they will enjoy. Commit yourself to searching for a job every weekday, and do not let your ego keep you from telling others that can help you about your job loss. You aren't the first person and you won't be the last person to lose their job. Nearly every working person has been fired or laid off at least once. Use all possible avenues to search for another job, which include newspaper ads, the internet, cold-calling companies, staffing companies, and word of mouth. Don't feel like a bum if a month goes by and you haven't been called in for an interview; search harder, something will come through. In the meantime, you can search for a job in any field just to pay your bills.

I became somewhat obsessive-compulsive after a month went by and I hadn't been called in for an interview. I checked job sites every half hour for new postings. I also became somewhat of a grump, as I would get irritated at friends who called me between nine and five because I was hoping they would be an employer. I was feeling particularly horrible one day when I drove by a person on the street selling framed poems. My eyes fell on one titled *Don't Quit*, and I laughed because I felt like I was supposed to see it. I realized then that it was only a matter of time before I got the job I needed, and worrying incessantly wasn't going to make it come faster.

Get Out of the House

Take advantage of all the extra free time you have to avoid being stressed out about your job loss. Read, exercise, do some of the things you couldn't when working 40 hours a week. Do not allow yourself to stay in the house pigging out, sleeping, watching television or being depressed.

Barnes & Noble became my best friend when I was looking for work, so did parks and matinee movies. And of course, when I eventually secured a job I missed all that time to myself, not to mention sleeping late.

Learn from the Experience

Whether you were laid off or fired, there is a lesson to be learned from the experience. Perhaps you learned what kind of company you don't want to work for ever again; situations with co-workers or your boss that led to your firing that you should avoid next time; or maybe losing your job made you realize how lucky you were to have it and you'll be more grateful and humble working on the next job. Everyone takes away something different that can help them be more successful. Whatever lesson you've learned, remember that your job loss can be a major turning point in your life—a positive turning point. Take time to reevaluate what kind of career you truly want, the direction you want to head in, and what you will need to accomplish to help you achieve your career goals.

After being fired/quitting, I spent months agonizing over what I could have done to save my job. But had I kept my mouth shut I would have also shut myself out of experiences I have been very fortunate to have. I truly believe that losing that one job set me on a totally different life path—a better path. Thus my getting fired turned out to be a blessing in disguise. The truth is that I probably never would have left that company on my own because I was just too comfortable. Sometimes you have to be kicked out of someplace in order to go where you need to be. As *Wall Street Journal* career columnist Hall Lancaster once wrote, "Getting fired is nature's way of telling you that you had the wrong job in the first place."

ILLEGALLY DISMISSED?

Sometimes it seems like it's easier to get fired than it is to get hired. Most firings never seem fair or just to the person getting dismissed, and many times people are fired for reasons that are hard to comprehend. What's worse, employers can virtually fire someone at-will because they know their employee is not protected by the law in most instances. You forgot to type that letter? Bye! You refuse to put your hair in a ponytail? See ya! You think our company policies are outdated? Go start your own company! Getting fired really is that easy. So, while many people's first thought is to sue their company for giving them the boot, the chance that they will win a lawsuit is very slim simply because the law is not on their side. Oftentimes, battling an employer is just not worth it because most people wouldn't opt to go back to the company that fired them anyway.

Yet the law is on the employee's side in certain situations. State and federal laws protect employees from being fired because of their ethnicity, age, national origin, religious beliefs, gender or because of a handicap. And although there is not a federal law prohibiting firing employees because of their sexual orientation, at least 15 states have made it illegal to discriminate (which often includes termination) against employees because of their sexual preference.

You may be fired because of someone else's prejudice during the course of your career because racism, sexism, ageism, and all those other uncool "isms" are still a problem in the workplace. If you feel that you were discriminated against and fired due to prejudice then you may have a case worth fighting for. Contact your local Equal Employment Opportunity Commission to discuss your case with a counselor, or seek advice from a lawyer who specializes in employment law.

Part 3
Real World Questions

Chapter 23

Where Should I Live?

"Toto, we're not in Kansas anymore."
—Dorothy, from the Wizard of Oz

Choosing where to live is yet another decision graduation often demands us to make. Do we stay put for a while, move back to our hometown, to a city we're familiar with, or one we've just seen on a map?

Moving from San Marcos, Texas to Houston after I graduated was not something I really had to think about. I had a great job awaiting me there, friends, family, a boyfriend, and it was a major city. So I was 100 percent confident that Houston was meant to be my home after finishing college—if only for a while.

A year later I was in a U-Haul headed from Houston to Fort Worth, Texas where I grew up. I was not especially happy about having to move back because of job loss, but the move had advantages and I had a plan. Through living with my mom, I could save up money to move to New York—a move I felt compelled to make. Also, most of my family lived in Fort Worth, including a soon-to-be born niece. So while I was not anxious to move from "H-Town" back to what I thought was appropriately nicknamed "Funky Town," I knew that the move made sense.

Yet when the time came for me to move to New York my stomach was doing tap dances. Even after all my plans had been finalized and I was sitting on a plane bound for the East Coast and a new life, I couldn't help but wonder if I was making the smartest decision. I was heading thousands of miles away from my family to a place notorious for cold weather, an exorbitant cost of living, rude people, crowded streets, and where the worst act of terrorism on American soil had recently taken place. What's more, I only knew one person who lived there. But, I reminded myself over and over again, it's also the publishing capital of the world; it's the most diverse city in America; there's tons to do at nearly all hours of the day; it's home to artists, singers, actresses, and NAS; and you're also going there to get your master's degree. So, in spite of my ambivalence, I decided not to ask the pilot to turn the plane around.

I lived in New York for three years, but I was only really comfortable living there the last two. I almost packed my bags and headed to the airport once or twice in the first few months that I was there. I was appalled at having to pay $950 for a 1 ½ bedroom apartment that was worth $450, seeing rodents in my super clean kitchen, and going grocery shopping and to the laundromat with my own store-bought cart. But I found strength in the knowledge that "if I could make it here, I could make it anywhere," and my certainty that New York was where I was supposed to be.

If you are thinking about moving to an entirely new city for career-related reasons, applaud yourself for your bravery. It takes guts and a lot of faith to move somewhere new. Apparently, the United States is filled with lots of brave people. According to the Census Bureau, more than six million people move each year for career-related reasons.

There will be pros and cons to any move you make, whether it is across town or across the nation. Make sure you've done your research on a city before you decide on taking that leap of faith. Consider the following factors:

1. *The People:* If the first thing you want to know before you go anywhere is "how many black folks are there?" then you may

find yourself miserable in a city where you can go days without seeing a black face. It doesn't make much sense to move to a place that doesn't have more than a handful of people you would feel comfortable spending your free time with. Find out the following information from the city's official website before you start packing your bags:
- The racial breakdown of the city.
- The male to female ratio.
- Age demographics.

2. Cost of Living: If the salary you're offered in a certain city seems unusually generous, the chances are it's not just because they like you—the cost of living may be exceptionally high. This means that the salary you receive may have less spending power than that offered by another company in a different city. Before moving to a city you know little about, compare the prices of certain things you know you'll need and have to pay for. Consider the following information:
- The cost of housing, including hotels and motels.
- The cost of car insurance and gas.
- Tax rates, including state, local, and property taxes.
- The cost of utilities, including electricity, water, gas and phone service.
- The cost of food at grocery stores, fast food places and restaurants.

3. The Job Market: How long you'll stay with a particular company is uncertain. If you move to a city just because of a job offer it's important to know that there will be other job opportunities in that same city should you decide to quit that job, but stay in the same location. Call the city's local Chamber of Commerce to find out the following information:
- How many companies like the one you may work for are in the city.
- The average salary for your occupation in the city.
- The unemployment rate, and the rate in your field in

that city.
- If there is growth in your field in that city.

4. *Housing:* Whether you have your own place or share a residence, housing costs can take a huge chunk out of your salary. The average cost of a one-bedroom apartment can vary by as much as $1,000 depending on what city and neighborhood you live in. The salary you receive should allow you to afford a low to moderately priced apartment or house in a relatively safe neighborhood, preferably no more than 30 miles from your job. Check the city's local newspaper to find the average prices for apartments and houses.

5. *Climate:* Think about your climate preferences and the city's average climate. Luckily, most U.S. city climates follow the normal pattern of having a spring, summer, fall and winter. But think about how happy you would be if you moved to one of those cities that stays extraordinarily cold, hot or rainy for longer than just three months, or suffered from droughts, hurricanes, tornadoes or earthquakes.

6. *Crime:* You don't want to be a single woman living in a city or neighborhood where people tell you to stay inside after dark. Talk to people in the community about how safe they feel living there. At nighttime visit the neighborhoods you are considering living in. You should also find out the following information from the police department or a website they can direct you to:
- The crime rate in the city and in the neighborhood you plan to live.
- What types of crimes occur most.
- The number and percentage of crimes during the last year against women.

7. *Education:* You never know when you will get the urge to get another degree or just take some interesting classes. You might hate having to commute to another city to do this. Check to see

if there are colleges or universities in the city that you can afford and would want to attend.

8. Recreation/Entertainment: You don't want to be bored out of your mind in a city, regardless of the money you're making. While you don't have to live in a major city that has tons to do at all hours, residing somewhere that has enough recreation and entertainment spots to fit your needs is important. Find out if there are an adequate amount of malls, movie theaters, museums, night clubs, restaurants, parks and libraries to fit your taste. If there are any particular activities you enjoy, such as going to dance classes, find out how many places offer them.

Chapter 24

Why Do I Have to Pay My Dues?

"In the business world, everyone is paid in two coins: cash and experience. Take the experience first; the cash will come later."
Harold Geneen

Wouldn't it be cool if we could just click our heels three times and be where we wanted to be in our careers? We could then skip the master's degree program, skip the internship, skip the entry-level job, skip the climb up the corporate ladder, and then skip on into a position that would have taken us years to secure by any other means than pure magic. All that matters is that we got to where we wanted to be anyway, right?

The thought of success, fame, and fortune makes many people's hearts beat faster, but the hard work, patience, and discipline it takes to acquire what we want often slows it down. During college many of us said we were going to be doctors, lawyers, famous writers and such, and halfway expected for those titles to just be bestowed upon us after graduation. It's no wonder that we're taken aback when the full realization comes that it'll be eight years before we're a doctor, six years before we're a lawyer, or too many to count before we're deemed a famous writer. All that in-between time is looked upon as a nuisance.

Sometimes we even treat the in-between time as a nuisance, and that's not good because we could be bothered for years. Turning our nose up at internships, assistant positions and more school, we act as if these are things we must endure. We might even feel that the work is beneath us. Get coffee? Take notes? Answer the phone? Assist *you*? Is this what we went to college for? we wonder.

I was indignant when the director of my master's program in publishing suggested that I get an internship when I could not find a job I wanted. I had been the managing editor of a newspaper and he wants me to get an internship? I fumed. But that was the problem. I had experience in newspaper publishing, and virtually none worth bragging about in books. Had I been a little more hard-headed, I might have really avoided getting an internship, but I did. It was at a literary agency and I loved it. No, I didn't have my own office, much less my own cubicle. And yes, I had to do administrative type work that I loathed by nature. However, I was opened up to another aspect of the publishing business, treated with respect and like an actual associate at the agency, and was mentored by the owners. Had I decided I was too good to have to "pay my dues," I would have been hurt by more than just my ego.

The reality of the situation is that graduating from college, even with a master's or doctorate degree, usually marks the beginning of our careers. This sometimes means long hours, more studying, not so great pay, and yes, getting coffee. Beginning means paying your dues, and not too many people are exempt from paying them. Regardless of what degree you've earned or your title, you'll likely be looked upon as a rookie on the job because you've just graduated.

It's just like being a freshman in college again. You had to take all those boring prerequisites before you could get into your major. You had to be a contributing member of an organization before you could run for president. And you definitely had to be inducted into a sorority before you could call yourself a soror. Likewise, you won't be able to stride into a new company, name your price, ask where your office is, start working on major league deals, and put up a "Head Black Woman in Charge" sign. "What has she accomplished?" "How many years has she been in the game?" "What are her credentials?" your co-workers will ask. They'll expect to be shown more than a degree.

If you find you have lots of dues to pay to get where you want then roll up your sleeves and put on a smile. Having a good attitude about the hard work ahead will make the days, months or years go by faster. Humbly accept every task that's required of you to get ahead in your career, realizing that your work is not in vain. You can learn career enhancing knowledge on any job if you go in with the right mindset.

I once called to check up on a friend who I knew was struggling somewhat in his career as a poet/business owner. Always the optimist, when I asked what he was up to, he replied, "Oh. Just working on my story." "Your story?" I asked, confused. "Yeah, all the stuff I'm going through now will make good story material for when I'm rich and famous and am being interviewed by reporters!" he said.

Like him, you're working on your story. No one will want to hear about how you graduated from college and were handed all that you wished for. Your friends won't mind listening, however, about how you patiently busted tables and babysat while holding down a full-time job to pay for graduate school. Your children will want to hear about the faith you had in yourself that helped you work your way up in a Fortune 500 company. Colleagues will want to learn how you went from delivering coffee to delivering paychecks you signed. And after recounting your adventures you can smile and say, "You know. . .success is a journey, not a destination. It's all about paying your dues."

Chapter 25

Should I Quit My Job?

"The return from your work must be the satisfaction which that work brings you and the world's need for that work. With this, life is heaven, or as near heaven as you can get. Without this—with work which you despise, which bores you, and which the world does not need—this life is hell."
—*W.E.B DuBois*

In today's society it's now common for people to work for more than 10 different companies in their lifetime. Given this fact, the chance that you'll retire from the first company you work for upon graduation is slim. Like many new grads you'll probably bounce from company to company as you try to get yourself together and figure out what you really want to do. Yet while changing jobs frequently is not looked down upon like it was decades ago, your decision to change jobs should not be made hastily. Many people just entering the workforce make a bad habit of job-hoping in search of that "perfect job." But before we rush to open every door that opportunity may be waiting behind, we should also take into account the door we are shutting behind us, and where we are trying to end up in the long run.

JOB HOPPING WITH SENSE

Ideally, each position you take should be one that increases your knowledge and skill set, preparing you for bigger and better things. Think of each job as a "career builder." If you jump from job to job without gaining the knowledge needed to further your career, you'll always be in the same position you were in when you took your very first job. It's fine to leave once you've learned all you can from working at a company and are ready to move on, or if you determine that a job is not going to further your career goals, but don't make the decision to quit prematurely and end up quitting the next one just as fast. If you're thinking about leaving your job you should also be thinking about what you honestly want to do with your career so that your next move will be a smart one.

If you enjoy working at your company but are contemplating leaving because of things that can be changed or improved, such as a low salary or unchallenging work, consider talking to your boss and asking him or her if the company can help meet your needs. You'd be surprised at what you can get when you just ask for what you want. When unsure about whether to change jobs weigh the advantages and disadvantages carefully. Look at Amiya's case, for example.

Amiya's Dilemma

Amiya had always dreamed of being a noted biological research scientist. After graduating summa cum laude from a public university with a degree in biology, she took a job as a research assistant at a prominent university/biomedical research center. She had received offers from several other research centers that offered her more money than the $45,000 she was currently getting paid, but she opted for this company because of its reputation, perceived chance of advancement and interesting research projects. The company would also pay for half of her graduate school tuition. She was really excited during her first three months of employment, but after working there for six months she got the itch to leave. She determined that she really wasn't getting paid what she was worth and she also wasn't getting the hands-on experience she had expected because one of the center's research projects got cancelled. Amiya noted that she had a lot of other opportunities to consider and one seemed particularly exciting. Other fellow biology graduates had told her how she could make more than $75,000 a year pitching pharmaceutical companies' new products to doctors. This job, they bragged, would give her unlimited income earning potential and the chance to travel within the United States and abroad. A scout for one of these companies who was looking for young African-Americans contacted Amiya and basically guaranteed her a job.

Before trying to make a decision, Amiya talked to her supervisor about her two needs that weren't being met.

To Amiya's surprise, her supervisor promised her a $5,000 raise in eight months because she knew that Amiya was underpaid, and she said more interesting work would be coming within weeks. She also told Amiya that she wanted her to stay and would do all that she could to help her career blossom.

Though this news excited Amiya, she still went ahead and weighed the pros and cons of leaving her present job to break into the pharmaceutical sales business.

Do I Stay?

Advantages
1. Excellent research facility.
2. Chance to meet top-notch influential doctors and research scientists.
3. They'll pay for half of my graduate school tuition.
4. Promise of professional advancement.
5. More money in eight months.
6. Stay in my field because I still want to be a sought after research scientist.

Disadvantages
1. Not making as much money as I could right now.
2. Have to be bored for a while.

Do I Go?

Advantages
1. Chance to make a lot more money.
2. Chance to travel.

Disadvantages
1. Might not make a lot more money because the job is commission based.
2. May hate the career (I'm really not a sales person).
3. May not get to travel to the places I want.
4. Won't get the experience I need to become a sought after research scientist.

After actually reviewing all that her present job had to offer she decided to stay. It was pretty clear that she had a good thing going even if the work was kind of boring at the moment. While waiting on the new research project she volunteered to help out in another department and decided to get an easy part-time job at night until she got the raise she was promised.

Of course, there will always be opportunities and offers elsewhere that we'd be foolish not to accept. And time is too short to waste our potential at a job we don't enjoy, or in a career that we know is wrong for us. So when you've looked at all your options and feel in your heart that it's time to leave, just do it and wave goodbye to your old co-workers. Daina's decision was easy to make.

Daina's Dilemma

After interning two years during college for a small public relations agency in New York City, Daina was offered a full-time salaried position as a public relations associate. She was ecstatic. It would have been hard to find anything more than an entry-level public relations job in New York and she was on great terms with everyone she worked with. But after working three more years at the agency she found herself getting bored. She really wasn't doing much more than she did when she interned and she wanted to work with the big name clients her company couldn't seem to get a hold of. She had made many contacts while at the agency and was about to start sending out resumes when one of her friends at a larger agency in Atlanta called her and said her public relations director wanted to meet her. Supposedly, she had heard great things about Daina's work and wanted to feel her out to see if she would fit in at her company.

Daina jumped on the opportunity and had an interview set up the next week in Atlanta on the weekend. The public relations director was very impressed with Daina's work and aspirations, offered her a job as a senior public relations associate—a job that was hard to get among people who already worked there.

Daina would get the chance to work with million dollar clients at a reputable company, travel, and enjoy the freedom of not having to live paycheck-to-paycheck. Daina was getting paid $40,000 a year, which left her broke every month in New York. This agency offered her $50,000 a year, which could be stretched a long way in Atlanta. Daina didn't have time to weigh the pros and cons of leaving—she was too busy packing to move to Atlanta. She turned in her two-weeks notice to her public relations director. He was sad to see her go, but he understood that this job could provide more opportunities for Daina to really make a name for herself in the public relations field. Daina left that PR agency for the new one without any doubt in her mind that she was doing what was best for her career.

WHEN YOU KNOW IT'S TIME TO GO!

Now, there are some jobs that we should consider leaving, and then there are others that demand we start sending out resumes immediately. Unfortunately, some jobs you take may look good under the "job description," but end up making you sick in the stomach for various reasons. You'll probably spend as much time at work as you do with the people you love, so it doesn't make sense to keep working at a place that has you frowning during half of your day. While you are still urged to think wisely before quitting a job, when the following scenarios arise you are urged to think twice about staying.

You Know It's Time to Go . . .

1. When you are ever physically, sexually, verbally or emotionally abused and the actions of the abuser go unpunished or are ignored by management.

2. When you feel like you need to take a drink each morning to get through your workday.

3. When the work you do is boring and unchallenging to the point that you can do it with your eyes closed and hands tied behind your back.

4. When you consistently get denied raises or promotions you feel you've earned.

5. When your boss hints that you may be happy somewhere else.

6. When the only friends you have at work are the office goldfish.

7. When you spend most of your time at work day-dreaming about quitting.

8. When you get your check late more than you get it on time.

9. When you're not getting paid anywhere near what you should be.

10. When everyone from the CEO to the secretary's assistant is an incompetent jerk.

Quitting Correctly

While the urge to run out your employer's door may be strong at times, it's wise for you to quit the "correct way." Most companies expect to receive two-weeks notice from employees so they will have a chance to delegate the work to someone else or replace the person leaving. By giving two-weeks notice you'll leave with a better chance of receiving a favorable reference and being reemployed if need be. Telling your employer verbally about your decision may suffice for part-time or semi-professional positions, but for professional positions you should provide your employer with a written letter stating your intentions. In this letter include the following:

- The last day you will be working.
- Whether you would like to continue health care coverage and how long.
- How you would like to receive your last paycheck.
- It may be helpful to provide your boss with positive words stating what you appreciated about the company.

Chapter 26

Do I Have to Get a Second Job?

"Make your work to be in keeping with your purpose."
—Leonardo Da Vinci

No one wants to have to do it. Working one job can be taxing enough. But if you find yourself having to borrow money from your parents every month, or going without real groceries for weeks at a time, you might want to look at taking on another job—part-time. I recommend taking on a part-time job (as opposed to just getting a better paying full-time one) when the chance for advancement and more money in the future is high at your present job, or you sincerely love your job but it just doesn't pay too well. If you do decide to spend some extra hours in work mode, then search for a job that:

1. Doesn't conflict with your other work schedule.
2. Is close to your place of residence and in a safe location (because you will most likely be working at night).
3. Pays a decent wage, not minimum wage.

4. Is interesting and can enhance your skill set in some way.

5. Won't wear you down and have you missing work in the morning.

You can always find want ads for typical part-time jobs like telemarketers, cashiers, customer service reps and waitresses, but there are other alternatives. Call up a company in your field that interests you and ask them if they have any part-time, freelance or temporary positions that will fit your schedule.

If you can't stand busting your butt on two different jobs don't despair, you may still have other options. One alternative is using some skill or talent you have to make some extra money on the side. Can you design web sites, brochures, business cards, flyers or logos? Would you make a good tutor? Ever thought of teaching others how to play an instrument or learn a style of dance? Are your friends and family always asking you to do their hair or nails for free? It might be time to start charging them for your services. Working part-time for yourself will allow you to bring in some extra money on your own time, and could possibly be the beginning of your own business.

Chapter 27

Do I Have to Go Back to School?

"An investment in knowledge always pays the best interest."
—*Benjamin Franklin*

My grandmother once told me that going back to school is never a bad decision, and I believe she's right. There is a huge difference between the average lifetime earnings of those with just a bachelor's degree compared to those with a postgraduate education. According to the most recent Current Population Survey, people with master's degrees make an average of $384,800 more during their lifetime than those with just a bachelor's degree; those with doctorates earn $1,128,420 more. Given the monetary advantage of attaining more than a bachelor's degree, I think a better question to ask is "When is it a good time to go back to school?"

Certain careers we plan to have, such as a lawyer or pharmacist, require further education. Generally, people who intend on getting into occupations requiring more instruction should enter their needed program shortly after they receive their first degree. Without the advanced degree they can be stuck in limbo.

Yet other occupations, such as a social worker or secondary teacher, are easier to attain and advance in with a post-grad degree, but aren't off limits without one. For these positions it may be wiser to work a year or two before becoming a student again. This way you will have acquired some professional experience, which will make you even more marketable once you receive a post-graduate degree. You may also be able to save money to pay for life's necessities if you aren't able to work full-time while attending school.

You should be picky about where you receive your post-graduate degree because all schools aren't equal. You will be investing at least two years of your life getting a master's degree and as many as seven years for a doctorate. Finding a school that will meet the majority of your needs during this time period is crucial.

What to look for:

1. A school with an accredited and great program: Find the school with the best program you are interested in that you can afford to attend. Remember, just because the university up the street from you offers a graduate degree like the one you're looking for, doesn't mean that is where you need to go. Find out if the program has been rated one of the best of its kind, or at least is considered a good program to go through by professionals in your field. Before applying, also contact the department's academic counselor and find out the following:

- The program's retention rate and the number that graduate each year.
- If any of the faculty are particularly well-known in the field.
- How the program differs from other similar ones.
- How closely the faculty works with students.
- The job placement rate of the program and examples

of places recent graduates are now working.
- Any recent awards/recognitions the program has received.

When you visit the school, ask to speak privately to at least two students in the program to find out their likes and dislikes. Also ask for the contact information of two recent alumni to get their opinion about the program.

2. A school in a good location: It's probable that you'll have to move to receive your post-graduate degree. While you could attend the same school you received your bachelor's from I wouldn't recommend it. The change of atmosphere will help you better adapt to other environments and you're more likely to meet new and different people. The location of the school you choose should:

- Be someplace you'll like to live. Even if the program is great you're not going to spend all your time in class. Choose a university in a city that you'll feel comfortable living in for a couple of years.
- Have a lot of companies that you can work or intern for. Some cities are known for certain industries, like Los Angeles, which is known for its entertainment industry, and Washington D.C., which is home to many public policy organizations. You want to be able to gain experience in your field while you're going to school, which is easier when the city has a lot of companies you'd be interested in working for.

3. A school that offers you some kind of fellowship or assistantship: Increasing your knowledge will probably mean increasing your debt. However, you shouldn't have to pay for your entire post-graduate degree with student loans. Choose a university that offers to pay all or part of your tuition or housing because of your academic background or in exchange for working at the school.

4. A school where you feel welcome and comfortable: Take into account your preferences in regards to the size of the school and its racial and gender makeup. Also ask about the culture of the program. Are students and faculty super competitive or do they make a point of helping each other and have a high level of camaraderie?

5. A school that has adequate resources and facilities: Make sure the program is adequately funded so you are likely to get continued financial assistance and other types of support. Check out the library, and computer and gym facilities to see if they will meet your needs.

After leaving my first job after college I chose to go back to school. I had majored in print journalism and sociology but decided that I now wanted to work in book publishing. There are only a couple of cities to go to if you seriously want to pursue a career in book publishing and New York City is the best one. While I was told that most people didn't have a master's in the field, and I didn't necessarily need one, I still thought earning a master's in publishing would benefit me. I knew very little about the industry, had no contacts, and didn't have enough money to move to New York without a job.

There were two universities that offered a master's in the field: Pace University and New York University (NYU). I was accepted to both. While NYU was a more respected institution, I wasn't offered a very good financial aid package. Pace offered me an assistantship that paid my tuition and allowed me to gain experience in the field through working for their university press; my decision was easy.

I learned a lot through the program and made great contacts and friends. My post-graduate degree also allowed me to secure positions I wouldn't have even been considered for with just a bachelor's degree, including as a faculty member at a university.

Chapter 28

Where Are My Friends?

> *"Depth of friendship does not depend on length of acquaintance."*
> —Rabindranath Tagore

Starting out in the real world is kind of like starting out at college—especially if you're in a new city with few friends. You might feel lonesome from time to time and a little uneasy about how you will be received by others. Yet after you get to know some people you should find the new city much more enjoyable.

Finding a group of people outside your work environment who you can consider friends is important. Developing friendships with uplifting women may especially make starting out all over again much easier.

However, unlike college, where you were probably surrounded by people your own age, potential friends are more spread out in the real world. There aren't any resident assistants to gather everyone up and have ice-breaking sessions. You won't see the same people everyday like you did in class, making it easier to forge friendships. You may have to search for people in the real world, and recognize possible friends you may bump into.

I met one of my closest friends, Ramona Crayton, after I graduated from college and was living in Houston. Because I worked as an editor/reporter, meeting new people every other day was inevitable, but I still found it hard to make friends because I was always on assignment. I had a boyfriend at the time, but still longed for a good group of female friends I could hang out with. The majority of my college buddies were at least four hours away.

One day I was covering the new initiatives of a black women's organization and had to interview one of the members to ask her how the organization helped to improve her life. She was much older than me, but didn't look it, and I guess she was surprised to see someone so young working as a reporter because she started questioning me about my occupation and life in the middle of what was supposed to be my interview. She was friendly and very funny and I remember thinking "I wish she was my friend" in the middle of the conversation. My interview session was the start of one of my most rewarding friendships. I soon had someone I could go out with occasionally and receive great advice from. And because she was in public relations and an expert at networking, I eventually made a lot of great contacts through her. As the friendship grew she became the big sister I never had—the kind who won't hang up on you if you call at 9 a.m. on a Saturday to talk about the great date you had the night before.

You won't make many new friends sitting at home on the couch complaining to your best friend in a different state that you don't have anyone to hang out with. You have to get up and get out of your apartment/house to meet people. If the thought of going out to eat, to conferences, and to parks by yourself unnerves you, you've got to get over it. It's time to truly become independent and take a proactive approach to meeting people. Explore your new territory like you are getting paid to visit new places, and you'll be surprised at the fun you can have by yourself and the people you'll meet.

Pick up a newspaper and browse the art and entertainment section, or look at the calendar of events. Go to the events that look interesting by yourself and explore different local hangouts that attract your attention. Ask your co-workers what places they enjoy going to and go with them if you're invited. Perhaps they will introduce you to some people outside of work.

The following is just a sample of places you can venture out to by yourself:

- Museums
- Parks
- Book stores
- Organizational meetings that interest you
- Movie theaters
- Plays
- Malls
- Church
- After hours venues
- Restaurants
- Parades
- Banquets
- Workshops
- Seminars

Of course, if you want to meet people you can't just wait for them to notice you. Sometimes you're going to have to initiate conversations. Remember that you can't expect people to talk to you if you look like you don't want to be spoken to. Always have a pleasant demeanor wherever you go. Your next best friend could be turning the corner.

Chapter 29

Is This It?

"You are not here merely to make a living. You are here in order to enable the world to live more amply, with greater vision, with a finer spirit of hope and achievement. You are here to enrich the world, and you impoverish yourself if you forget the errand."
—Woodrow Wilson

Even the most fulfilling jobs can leave us asking the "Is this it?" question at the end of the work day. Work, eat and sleep—is this it? Get my paycheck twice a month—is this it? Have some good days and some bad ones—is this it? Is this what I'm supposed to do for the rest of my adult life? Is this what I went to college for—to save up for retirement?

While getting started in your career you may find that much of your time is spent just getting used to working for a living. Still, the "is this it?" feeling can begin to creep into your heart very early on.

While some people may tell you with downcast eyes and a smirk, "Yep, this is about it," the truth is that whether this is going to be about it or not depends on you.

Ask yourself how you perceive your job and your career. Why are you waking up to an annoying alarm clock five days out of the week? If you're doing it just to pay the bills, or because your mom, dad and the rest of the working world told you "everyone works," then sooner or later you'll be asking the question "is this it?" too.

But if you view your job as a powerful and enjoyable tool to living out your dreams, and if you understand that your career is just a part of what hopefully is and will continue to be an interesting and exciting life, then the baffling "is this it?" question may evolve into "what else is there?"

What else will enrich my life? What else will help give my life meaning? What else will help me fulfill my purpose? What else can I look forward to in the morning? The funny thing is that there's an endless amount of "what elses" in the world—so if you dedicate your life to seeking out beneficial things to be a part of, you'll never even think to ask the "is this it?" question.

You have to seek out adventures, no matter how big or small, that appeal to you and warrant your time and energy. Look at the broader picture of your life, beyond work and bills. Ask yourself what else you can be doing at this point in time to bring you more enjoyment. If they have the time and some extra change, some people travel. Others enrich someone else's life through volunteering. Do you have a hobby or rarely used talent—drawing, writing, choreography, singing, ice-skating? Cultivate that hobby or talent and use it to inspire others or make some extra money. Is there an issue you feel strongly about—abused and neglected children, the homeless, the waste of tax payer's money, voter apathy, black American's lack of economic empowerment? Talking about the situation won't change it, but getting involved in the cause can change you and society. There are thousands of things you can be a part of besides your employer's staff. Seek out those things and consider them just as important as your job, and even more so for your sense of well-being and purpose.

Part 4
Handling Real World Barriers

Chapter 30

Handling Racial Discrimination in the Workplace

"I never doubted my ability, but when you hear all your life that you're inferior, it makes you wonder if the other group has something you never seen before. If they do, I'm still looking for it."
—Hank Aaron

African-Americans have continually proven that we can compete on any playing field with white Americans, as well as people of other ethnicities. In the courtroom, the hospital, the classroom, the boardroom, and even in space—we have shown that we have the drive and the intelligence to succeed in any workplace. So it's sad that in some workplaces people still feel that we must prove ourselves to them. Yet perhaps what's even sadder is that we have to prove anything to anyone.

Overcoming racial discrimination on the job may be the hardest obstacle you'll ever have to face in your career. And though it is possible that you won't ever encounter racial discrimination in the workplace, it is just as possible that you will.

American employers of all sizes and in all industries have a poor record of providing a work environment free of racial discrimination. Evidence of this is the 27,411 race-based charges that were filed with the Equal Employment Opportunity Commission (EEOC) in fiscal year 2005 (October 2004 through September 2005); approximately 82.5 percent of these filings were by African-Americans.

Despite the passage of the Civil Rights Act of 1964, and the million dollar lawsuits that result from cases of discrimination, companies still continue to defy the law, morality and reason.

Yet, unlike African-Americans of past generations, who perhaps didn't feel empowered enough to combat racial discrimination in the workplace, African-Americans in today's workforce are able to more effectively confront and handle such bigotry.

Individuals in your workplace can discriminate against you in a variety of ways. Some are not very obvious. But knowing some of the signs can better help you recognize discrimination when it occurs.

Possible Signs of Discrimination

- *Being denied or not considered for promotions you deserved:* Your supervisor will not give you a reason why you were denied or looked over for a promotion, and perhaps promotes someone who is less qualified than you. You may also notice that other African-Americans are denied well-deserved promotions or are slow to get them.
- *Being given easier assignments than your white counterparts:* Your supervisor gives you easy assignments that you are overqualified to handle, and gives less experienced white employees more challenging tasks.
- *Being given harder assignments than your white counterparts:* Your supervisor gives you assignments that you aren't trained for and is unwilling to train you, while training white employees and giving them simpler assignments. You may then be punished for your poor performance.

- *Being made to take tests you shouldn't have to:* You're required to take tests that white employees with your position and experience don't have to.
- *Being given menial tasks outside your job description:* Being given menial tasks (even like cleaning the bathroom) for which you're overqualified or that doesn't have anything to do with your job, while white employees aren't asked to do the same tasks.
- *Being given "behind the scenes" assignments:* Your supervisor gives you assignments that offer little recognition or in which you are neither seen or heard, while white employees of equal standing with you get assignments that bring more recognition.
- *Being excluded from important meetings:* Your supervisor doesn't invite you to, or denies your entrance to meetings that someone in your position should attend.
- *Being ignored:* Your supervisor ignores your questions, suggestions and solutions, treating you with less respect than white employees.
- *Being monitored closely:* Your supervisor monitors you more closely than white employees without explaining why.
- Being called derogatory names.
- Being the subject of racist jokes.
- Being the subject of racist comments.
- Being made to listen to racist jokes.
- Being made to listen to racist comments.
- Being asked racist questions.
- Being discouraged from interacting with clients.

You may come upon a situation in which you can't be certain that you're being treated differently or unfairly because of your race. This is a baffling problem when attempting to confront racial discrimination at work. You don't want to offend someone for their innocent mistake by accusing them of being a racist. But you also don't want to disregard anything just because you're uncertain. Not confronting discrimination can be just as stressful as letting your grievances be known.

The following are steps you can take when faced with racial discrimination.

Confronting Racial Discrimination on the Job

1. Identify the problem: Determine exactly how you're being discriminated against, and make sure you have all the facts to show it by keeping a log of each occurrence.

2. Get a Second Opinion: Find someone within your work environment that you can confide in and get his or her input. It is possible that there could be other reasons besides your race for the problems you are experiencing. If you don't feel comfortable speaking with anyone at your job, then talk to someone outside your job whose opinion you trust. You can also speak with representatives of the EEOC or NAACP.

3. Confront the offender: Talk to the person you have a problem with, be it another employee or your supervisor. Calmly state the problems you perceive and ask for an explanation for his/her actions. At this point there is no need for you to bring up race as the central issue, unless there is no other way around it (i.e, you've heard someone refer to African-Americans in a derogatory way). The person's actions should be the central issue.

Example: "I noticed that the company policy is that sales reps cannot start working with customers unless they make a passing score of 70 on their assessment test, and you have said this verbally as well. However, when I had to take my test you told me that I would need to make a score of 90 to work with customers. Is there a reason why I was treated differently?"

* This tactic works best if a co-worker or immediate supervisor is doing the discriminating. You have a bigger problem to tackle when treating African-Americans unjustly seems to be a part of the company's culture.

4. File a complaint: If the problem isn't resolved or it's clear that racial discrimination is a problem throughout the company, you should file a formal complaint with the company and talk to the owner or manager about the problems you see. Remember that they have a legal responsibility to end the existing racial discrimination.

5. Report the business: If the problem isn't resolved or the situation worsens, report the business and file a complaint with the EEOC.

You might find yourself under even more stressful times if you're still working at the company when a lawsuit or an investigation takes place. Whether you decide to stay throughout the ordeal is a personal choice. By staying you're taking even more of a stand. However, you may also be helping to keep a company that's not going to change in business.

Just remember that racial discrimination isn't something that you have to or should endure. When you allow others to treat you differently or unfairly you send a signal that their actions are acceptable and understandable. Yes, confronting racial discrimination can be tough. You can lose your job, contacts, and sour your reputation among some people. But in the process you help uphold justice and uncover racists who don't deserve their positions. You also make the dream of working in an environment free of racial discrimination closer to becoming a reality.

Overcoming Ignorance

Stereotypes of African-Americans (and people of all ethnicities) abound, and people in your workplace may assume things about you because of your skin tone. Because of this, it's possible that people may say and do things to you that are inappropriate out of ignorance, and not out of spite caused by racism.

I have been told by white, Asian, and Hispanic co-workers that I don't "act black." I still don't know what that means. I never get angry when I hear that weird statement; I just let whoever said it know that it was not a compliment, and there is no such thing as "acting black," or white, Asian or Hispanic for that matter.

A white manager once expressed his surprise that I was listening to The Dave Matthews Band. "Don't you like rap?" he wanted to know. I politely informed him that black people can have other musical tastes besides rap, and besides, white boys buy more rap music than anyone.

In short, don't take everything people say or do as an insult. Instead, use incidents like mine to educate people. It's useless to berate someone who should have, but didn't, know better. You may end up coming off as easily agitated and uptight—a common criticism of black people working in predominantly white environments.

Also be mindful that being black doesn't prevent you from being labeled a racist. So watch what you do and say. When working with a diverse group, you need to be more understanding and sensitive of cultural differences, and how one's ethnicity helps shape the way one thinks about issues, other people and the world. But you also must realize that people are people. No one likes assumptions made about them because of their ethnicity. And even the most playful of co-workers often detest jokes and naïve statements made about their culture or ethnicity.

Chapter 31

Handling Sex Discrimination & Sexual Harassment in the Workplace

"In my world, black women can do anything."
—Julie Dash

You know you're as smart, hard-working, diligent and ambitious as any of the men you work alongside. You have all the makings of a successful employee, and if given the same opportunities as the men you work with there's no limit to what you can achieve for a company and for yourself.

So why do you get the impression that you aren't being given the same opportunities as the men you work with? Why does it seem like you aren't taken as seriously as your male counterparts? Why do you get the sickly feeling that you're being discriminated against in various ways solely because of your sex? Perhaps it's because you are.

If you get the inclination that you are being treated differently or unfairly on the job because you lack a certain part of the male anatomy, chances are you're right. Sex discrimination is a common practice in all industries and can happen at any company. It is such a prevalent problem that it's prohibited under Title VII of the Civil Rights Act of 1964.

Sex discrimination appears in many forms. The clearest example of sex discrimination lies in the wage gap existing between male and female employees. According to the Equal Employment Opportunity Commission (EEOC), on average, women currently make about 75 cents for every dollar a white male makes even when we have the same position, job duties and background. We, as African-American women, fare far worse. It's estimated we currently make about 66 cents for every dollar a white male makes.

One might think that women who hold jobs that pay very well and require more education would have a better shot at receiving equal pay, but the opposite is true. A study by Hilary Lips, a Radford University psychology professor, found that only women making between $25,000 to $30,000 a year are likely to receive equal pay. On average, female lawyers and judges earn about 69 cents for every dollar a man earns, female financial managers earn 63 cents for every dollar a man is paid, and female physicians earn a paltry 59 cents for every buck their fellow male physicians take home.

Pay inequity occurs despite the fact that the Equal Pay Act of 1963 makes it illegal for employers to pay unequal wages to men and women who perform jobs that require substantially equal skill, effort and responsibility, and that are performed under similar working conditions within the same establishment. The EEOC received approximately 970 equal pay act charges for fiscal year 2005; the majority of these filings were by women.

Beyond not receiving pay equal to men, women may encounter other discriminatory practices, which include:

- Not being hired because of our sex.
- Being made to take tests that aren't required, or having to score higher than men on tests.

- Not being considered for promotions.
- Being given easier assignments than men.
- Being given menial assignments or jobs traditionally thought to be "women's work," such as answering the phones, filing and typing—even when this is not in our job description.
- Being given "behind the scenes" assignments that offer little recognition.
- Being excluded from important meetings.
- Being ignored when we offer suggestions and solutions.
- Being monitored more closely than men.

What would possess someone to treat you like this because you were born female? Mainly insecurity. Despite all the contributions women have made in every field men have traditionally occupied (which is nearly every field), some men and women still hold false beliefs about women in the workplace. Stereotypes/beliefs include:

- Women can't handle pressure like men can.
- Women can't make decisions as fast as men can.
- Women can't learn skills as fast as men can.
- Women can't think as critically as men can.
- Women can't lead others as well as men can.
- Women can't solve problems as well as men can.
- Women belong at home, not in the workforce.
- Women should not compete and take jobs away from men because men are the breadwinners for the family.

The good news is that women of all ethnicities and ages are refusing to let sex discrimination go unpunished. Companies have a legal responsibility to ensure that women aren't treated unfairly on the job, by anyone. Approximately 23,094 sex discrimination charges were filed with the EEOC for fiscal year

2005, and nearly 20 percent of those complaints were filed by black women.

The WAGE Project, Inc., an organization established to end discrimination against women in the American workplace, compiled a list of various sexual discrimination lawsuits filed against employers. The following are some of the lawsuits:

$ . . . Boeing agreed to settle a class-action gender discrimination lawsuit in 2004 covering 29,000 women in the Puget Sound-area of Washington who worked for Boeing between 1997 and 2004. The class action lawsuit was brought by 12 plaintiffs. The women charged that they were denied access to lucrative overtime work and promotions along with discrimination in compensation. The lawsuit claimed that Boeing denied its female employees job assignments, promotional opportunities, management positions, training, equal pay, overtime, tenure, comparable retention ratings, bonuses, and other benefits and conditions of employment because of their gender. Plaintiffs argued that Boeing's various compensation, promotion and overtime decision-making practices were tainted with "excessive" subjectivity and managerial discretion and that the absence of objective, empirically measurable standards worked systematically to disadvantage female employees. The plaintiff further alleged that Boeing failed to take action to eliminate the statistical disparities between men and women's salaries. In order to resolve the lawsuit, Boeing agreed to a consent decree, but it didn't admit any fault or wrongdoing. Under the terms of the settlement, Boeing has agreed to pay between $40.6 million and $72.5 million, to be divided among the plaintiffs, other members of the class, and class attorneys.

$ . . . In 2001, the first sex discrimination suit ever brought against the Gardena City, Calif. Police Department resulted in a $1.65 million award to Dianne Elliot, who served the department for 14 years. Elliot, who was the department's first female sergeant, claimed she was repeatedly passed over for promotion because of her gender and then retaliated against when she complained. In 1995, she began seeking promotion to the rank of lieutenant. Elliot alleged that despite exemplary reviews and top test scores, she was repeatedly denied the lieutenant's post, and when she complained about it to her supervisors, they began issuing reprimands concerning her job performance. Her supervisors also allegedly interrogated Elliot's subordinates and finally placed her on administrative leave.

$ . . . In 2000, Karen E. Simmons-Beathea charged that she was fired by the Baltimore Cable Access Corporation (BCAC) in retaliation for her complaint of sex-based wage discrimination. Simmons-Beathea claimed she was paid significantly less than male counterparts in the industry and 20 percent less than a less experienced man who was hired as her successor to do the same job. Simmons-Beathea was awarded $45,000 in a consent decree.

$ . . . Morgan Stanley agreed to settle a class-action sex discrimination lawsuit in July 2004. The EEOC filed the lawsuit against the major securities firm on behalf of 340 women for sex discrimination that occurred in Morgan Stanley's Institutional Equity Division world wide ("IED"). The suit alleged that women were denied promotions, women received unequal pay, and women were discriminated against in the terms and conditions of their employment. The EEOC also alleged that Morgan Stanley retaliated against the lead plaintiff Alison Schieffelin and other women when they tried to assert their rights. Morgan Stanley will pay out a total of $54 million according to the terms of the consent decree.

$ . . . In 2000, the EEOC and George Junior Republic (GJR), a residential home for boys committed by the courts for rehabilitation, settled a lawsuit filed under Title VII of the Civil Rights Act of 1964. The EEOC alleged that at least six female employees were paid lower wages than their male counterparts and then were retaliated against and subjected to a hostile work environment because they complained about the wage discrepancy. The female employees were denied the same opportunities to work overtime and to obtain additional assignments as were provided to male counselor parents. Five women were forced to resign because of intolerable working conditions. GJR agreed to pay the women $280,000.

For more information about The WAGE Project, Inc. visit www.wageproject.org.

If you find you're being discriminated against because of your gender, there are steps you can take to remedy the problem.

Confronting Sex Discrimination on the Job

1. Identify the problem: Determine exactly how you're being discriminated against, and make sure you have all the facts to show it by keeping a log of each occurrence and written documents or voicemails that can be used as evidence.

2. Get a Second Opinion: Find another woman in your work environment that you can confide in and get her input. It's possible that there could be other reasons besides your sex for the discrimination you believe is occurring.

3. Confront the offender: Talk to the person you have a problem with. Calmly state your case and ask/demand that the discrimination end. This works best if a co-worker is doing the discriminating or an immediate supervisor. When discriminating against women seems to be a part of the company's culture, you have a bigger problem on your hands.

4. File a complaint with the company: If the problem isn't resolved or it's clear that sex discrimination is a problem throughout the company, you should file a formal complaint with the company and talk to the owner or manager about the problems you see. Remember that they have a legal responsibility to end the existing sex discrimination.

5. *File a complaint with outside agencies:* If the problem isn't resolved or the situation worsens, report the business and file a complaint with the EEOC.

HANDLING SEXUAL HARASSMENT

Sexual harassment is just as prevalent as sex discrimination in the workplace and is prohibited under Title VII of the Civil Rights Act of 1964. The EEOC received approximately 12,679 charges of sexual harassment for fiscal year 2005; only 14.3 percent of those charges were filed by men. According to the EEOC, unwelcome sexual advances, requests for sexual favors, and other verbal or physical conduct of a sexual nature constitute sexual harassment when this conduct explicitly or implicitly affects an individual's employment, unreasonably interferes with an individual's work performance, or creates an intimidating, hostile or uncomfortable work environment.

The WAGE Project, Inc., an organization established to end discrimination against women in the American workplace, compiled a list of various sexual harassment lawsuits filed against employers. The following are some of the lawsuits:

$ . . . A federal jury ordered Boulder, Colorado-based Paladin Press to pay $100,000 in 2004 to a former employee for sexual harassment. The award to Marilyn Ranson includes $50,000 in compensatory damages and $50,000 in punitive damages. According to Ms. Ranson, the company president sometimes walked around the office wearing only a towel and made unwanted sexual advances toward her and other female employees, including asking female employees to kiss him when he handed out bonus checks at the holiday office party. Ms. Ranson also said that the president of the company commented after she had a baby that she looked so good he would make her pregnant again. The jury found that the alleged sexual conduct created a hostile working environment.

$ . . . Nielsen & Bainbridge, LLC, a manufacturer and distributor of containers and laminated foam boards, subjected four black female production workers to harassment based on sex and race. Both supervisors and co-workers participated in the harassment, including exposing their buttocks and genitalia, referring to women as "bitches" and "black hairy dogs" and, on two occasions, opening the restroom door when a female worker was using the toilet and throwing water on her. In a 2004 consent decree, the company agreed to pay the four women $155,000.

$ . . . The EEOC's largest sexual harassment settlement ever in the state of New York was reached in April 2003 for $5.425 million and significant remedial relief on behalf of a class of female workers at Lutheran Medical Center, a hospital based in Brooklyn, New York. The EEOC alleged that Dr. Conrado Ponio, during his employment at Lutheran, abused his authority by sexually harassing a class of female employees when conducting employment related medical examinations. The suit claimed that Mr. Ponio touched the employees' breasts and genital areas and made comments about their sexual and dating habits. He told the women that if they did not consent to everything he asked, they would not be hired.

$ . . . The former president of New Boston Select Staffing was awarded more than $666,000 in compensatory damages and $1.5 million in punitive damages in 2002 after she claimed the chairman of her employer's parent company sexually harassed her and fired her when she verbally complained. The plaintiff also charged that the company retaliated against her after she submitted a written complaint by asserting that she had quit and suing her for making improper financial commitments on behalf of the company, knowing she was about to resign.

$ . . . A federal jury in Colorado awarded $1 million in 2002 to the former business development manager of a Denver car dealership who claimed she suffered sexual harassment on the job for nearly four years. The plaintiff alleged that she was subjected to pinching, kissing, sexually explicit comments and was the target of false, sexually explicit rumors while employed by Chesrown Chevrolet.

$ . . . Dial, a manufacturer of soap products, allegedly engaged in a pattern or practice of sexual harassment and sex-based harassment against a group of current and former female employees at its Montgomery, Ill. facility, beginning around July 1988. The women alleged that male co-workers and supervisors propositioned them for sex, groped them and called them derogatory names. Pornography was allegedly circulated and posted in the plant, and some female employees felt "stalked" by male employees both at the plant and after work. Harassment allegedly occurred in the presence of supervisors who did nothing and sometimes engaged in the misconduct. The EEOC claims that Dial failed to document and investigate complaints of harassment and took little meaningful action to end the misconduct of its male employees. The EEOC identified approximately 90 women who were harassed while employed at Dial. The EEOC initiated a lawsuit against Dial Corporation on May 20, 1999. Dial agreed to resolve the lawsuit through a consent decree, but it did not admit any fault or wrongdoing. The consent decree provided for payment of $10 million in compensatory damages to eligible claimants.
*For more information about The WAGE Project, Inc. visit www.wageproject.org.

Even though the law provides a working definition for sexual harassment it can still be hard to identify. Even women may not be able to agree on what really constitutes sexual harassment because sometimes it boils down to what makes each of us feel uncomfortable. For example, it's obvious that you're being sexually harassed if a co-worker or boss purposefully touches your breasts, demands sex from you on your lunch break, or talks about how much he wants to make love to you. But what about if he just talks about how sexy you are every day and how much he wants to date you? Some women would just find his advances annoying and tolerate them; others might find his actions intolerable and file a complaint.

I worked for a respected publishing company whose owner was blatantly guilty of sexual harassment, yet I don't think anyone, including me, filed a complaint or sued. The owner was a witty, smart, elderly man who had recently suffered a stroke. His children now mostly managed the business, but he still attended meetings and could be seen often around the company. It seems that along with leaving him in a wheelchair, the stroke left him prone to say some rather inappropriate things. One day when I was bending over to browse for books on a low bookshelf he came upon me in his wheelchair. I heard him behind me and cringed because I knew he was looking at my butt. He had already commented on my physique at least six times in department meetings. Before I could straighten up he said, "Chaz, you look even more beautiful from behind." I turned around, looked at him like he had lost his mind, and walked away.

I talked to one of my co-workers about his actions and she recounted a handful of incidents involving other people, including herself. She said one day while he was whispering something in her ear he licked her earlobe.

Why didn't anyone say anything? I think it was because while he did make us feel uncomfortable, none of us ever felt threatened by him. We also felt sorry for him because he suffered a stroke that left him bereft of good judgment sometimes. And the man had built an absolutely wonderful place to work; no one wanted to hurt the company by filing a lawsuit. So the women who he bothered dealt with the situation by just walking the other way when they saw him coming or by ignoring his questionable comments when they couldn't escape being around him. However, if any of us had wanted to lodge a lawsuit we probably would have had a fairly good case.

It's likely that you'll know when someone is behaving in a manner that deserves to be ignored, confronted or punished through a complaint or lawsuit. If you feel you are being sexually harassed, by men or women, you can follow the same steps outlined in Confronting Sex Discrimination on the Job. You don't have to accept being made to feel like a sexual object or toy.

Whether you decide to stay with the company while the sex discrimination or sexual harassment issue is being resolved is a personal decision. Just keep in mind that staying with the company can be quite difficult if you're ignored or treated harshly by your bosses or the men or women angry with you. Also remember that you should work for a company where you feel respected. At companies where sex discrimination seems to be a part of its framework, it's likely that biases against women will remain even if the discrimination does stop due to complaints or lawsuits. So is the case for widespread sexual harassment. By continuing to work for this type of company you are helping to keep it in business.

SEXISM OR CHIVALRY?

Some men and women may believe they are doing you a favor by treating you differently because of your gender. These people would never intentionally do anything they thought was sexist. A manager might think he is doing you a favor as a woman by giving you an easier workload or allotting you shorter work hours. That's why it's important to express your dismay and find out the reason you're being treated differently, rather than just assuming it's being done on purpose to halt your growth or demean you.

Chapter 32

Handling the Naysayers

"Keep away from people who try to belittle your ambitions. Small people always do that, but the really great make you feel that you, too, can become great."
—*Mark Twain*

Your family and friends' questions seem appropriate enough, but you can't figure out why they have to bombard you with them. It's gotten to the point that you're beginning to despise the words "what," "why" and "how." "What makes you think you can be successful in that profession?" they ask with a frown. "Why would you want to move all the way out there?" "How are you going to live off of that amount of money?"

Their statements (repeated so many times you have all of them memorized) are even more bothersome. "You're living in a dream world if you think it'll be that easy." "It's going to take you forever to rise up in that company," they say. But you dismissed those questions and comments. Well, you had dismissed them until their litany of discouraging words made you start to rethink your plans. After all, your loved ones wouldn't question career choices you feel strongly about unless you were really heading in the wrong direction, right?

Wrong. Only your heart and your creator can lead you in the right direction. Other people can push you towards the path you need to take, but at the same time they can also push you backwards onto a road going nowhere if you allow them. You begin taking those backward steps the moment you start questioning your career goals and dreams because of someone else's fear of change, failure or success. But instead of letting certain people call you naïve and reckless for setting your sights high, you have to call these people out for what they are. These people are naysayers. Naysayers stand in your way of success.

Our society is filled with naysayers bent on telling people why they should settle for less than what they desire and deserve. What's worse is that sometimes it's our most cherished family and friends that offer us frowns and discouraging words instead of the smiles and good wishes we hope for.

Yet this is not unusual. Most people who consider themselves successful will tell you that they didn't get all the pats on the back they expected as they strove for that success. They received unconstructive criticism, crazy looks, and a whole heap of whys instead of why nots. And they got this from the people whose opinion mattered the most—their mom, dad, grandparent, sibling, teacher, aunt, uncle, best friend, mentor and significant other. But they're where they are today because they had the courage to ignore their naysayers instead of ignoring themselves. That is so very hard to do.

When faced with important decisions we want to have the support of others. We want to be cheered for and bragged on for taking the initiative to better ourselves. But we have to realize that sometimes those cheers and bragging words just aren't going to come. More importantly, we have to realize that a lack of support doesn't mean we're making the wrong decision. It simply means we're making a decision that someone else would not make. That's okay because we have our own lives to live.

A couple of my family members admonished me for planning to move to New York. I remember one of them asking how a "little ol'" thing like me was going to survive in that "horrible place." Nevermind that this person had never set foot on the East Coast. Instead of working in the publishing industry, I was advised to stay in Texas and become a high school teacher. From my family member's standpoint, working as a teacher would guarantee me job security, a steady paycheck, and keep me from moving across the country to a place he was afraid would be riddled with more terrorist attacks. I eventually did go into teaching—on the college level—but at the time this is not what I wanted. I think the worst kind of teacher is one who teaches out of necessity instead of love. If I had stayed and taught I would have spent more time daydreaming about the life I could have had in New York than educating students.

Whether you're venturing into a male-dominated field, quitting a good paying job you despise for a lower paying one you love, or moving across the country to pursue your career, don't let anyone's doubts stand in the way of your ambitions. Of course you should listen to those you trust and respect. It's wise to take heed of all the warnings you are given. But then you have to ask yourself what you want. The question should be what will make you content and proud. Envision the future you can have if you do what is necessary to achieve your career goals. And then, despite what the naysayers say, go after what you have envisioned.

Pointers on Overcoming the Naysayers

1. Make Up Your Mind: Naysayers cause us so much trouble because we're still waiting for their approval and blessings. We feel like our decision has to be justified by someone else in order for it to be the right one. We wouldn't feel this way if we would just make up our minds about what we're going to do, and then stick to that decision.

2. Don't Ask Naysayers Anything: We usually know how someone is going to respond to something. So why do we ask people we know will give us a negative response for advice? Don't ask naysayers how they feel about such and such or what they think and what they would do. You open yourself up to negativity by asking the wrong people for advice.

3. Surround Yourself With Positive People: Positive people may tell you they think you're heading in the wrong direction, but they will offer you their support anyway. You should gravitate toward and surround yourself with these people. Negative people, however, will shoot down your decisions and continue to criticize you even after they know you've made up your mind. If you can't remove negative people from your life then at least avoid them while you're trying to make an important decision.

4. Ask For Support: Ask for the support you're seeking from the naysayers you need support from. Tell them that you're not seeking their advice or approval; you just want and need their unconditional support. This may soften them up a little.

Chapter 33

Handling Self-doubt & the Fear of Failure

"It is impossible for a people to rise above their aspirations. If we think we cannot, we most certainly cannot. Our greatest enemy is our own defeatist attitude."
—Robert Williams

The most powerful and influential barrier to your success is someone you thought wanted the best for you. She's a woman you've confided all your hopes and dreams to and trusted with your life. If there wasn't anyone else you could rely on when times got tough you knew you could depend on her. Yet she has still betrayed your confidence time and time again, and if you don't acknowledge the power she has over you she may prevent you from creating the life you desire for yourself. Who would do such a thing? You would. A doubtful and fearful you, who is so scared to fail that you keep yourself from succeeding.

When you are overcome with self-doubt and the fear of failure you can become a barrier to your success. That frustrated voice inside your head that tells you the goals you're working towards can't be accomplished, and you're not good enough, smart enough, pretty enough, talented enough, and woman enough to accomplish them anyway, can be more detrimental to your livelihood than racism, sexism and ageism combined.

Feelings of self-doubt and the fear of failure aren't foreign to anyone. These two cousins of discouragement strike people at various points in their lives, usually when there is something they're hoping to achieve.

These negative feelings are what kept many of your high school classmates from going to college. They caused some of the people who entered college with you to drop out. Self-doubt and the fear of failure even managed to keep students who stayed in college from majoring in what they wanted to because they felt the classes would be too hard for them. What have the spirits of self-doubt and the fear of failure kept you from accomplishing thus far?

I still hate to admit this, but my self-doubt and fear of failure led me to leave New York after I had only been there a year and move to Atlanta. I became engaged to a man that lived there, and I used the engagement as an excuse for me to move. But the truth was that I didn't have the job I wanted, I was tired of paying sky-high rent, I was lonely, and I was frustrated to the point that I didn't see things getting better soon. "Soon" to me then meant within a month, as I can be ridiculously impatient. And I guess that somehow my unconscious reasoned that if I stayed and my situation didn't improve then I would be a failure; but if I left now then I had nothing to feel sorry about. So I left. And leaving New York at that time is the most foolish decision I have ever made in my life. I sold all my furniture, gave up my apartment, and moved to a state where it would be even harder for me to find a job in publishing.

It took me less than three days to realize what an awful mistake I had made, and why. I was a nervous wreck. When the UPS man brought my boxes to my fiancé's house I asked him if there was any way he could just have them shipped back. He looked at me like I was insane, and I sat right down in front of him in the driveway and started crying. The poor man probably thought I was being beaten.

Luckily, I wasn't silly enough to stay in order to avoid the embarrassment moving back to New York would bring. And I was thoroughly embarrassed. The majority of my family, friends and co-workers had told me the move would all but murder my career. My grandma was so mad she wouldn't talk to me. My friends called me back-to-back up until the time I boarded the plane to see what I was smoking.

What they hadn't known, of course, was that I had begun doubting my ability to have the career I envisioned. But I was finally able to recognize that by moving to Atlanta I was failing myself, not saving myself. Three weeks later I was back in New York, minus my own apartment, furniture, a job, and a fiancé. I did have a renewed sense of determination, faith and purpose, however, and I soon discovered that was all I needed.

If you're not careful you can sabotage your career by letting self-doubt and the fear of failure take control of your mind. They're sneaky and always waiting for an opportunity to do you harm. It doesn't matter whether the opportunity is big or small. Self-doubt and the fear of failure will keep you from applying for a position because it may be too difficult. Self-doubt and the fear of failure will stop you from trying to move up in a company because you might not fit in with management. If you allow them to, self-doubt and the fear of failure will talk you out of pursuing the career you dreamed of since you were a child because of your skin color and gender. They'll come up with a thousand reasons on why you can't and shouldn't attempt something to further your career as they destroy it in the process. Their scheming never stops. So while opportunity after opportunity may knock at your door, you may never hear it because self-doubt and the fear of failure are clogging your ears with nonsense.

If the spirits of self-doubt and the fear of failure are working in your life it's time they found another home. The belief that you can do anything you set your mind to is not a pipe dream.

The belief that everyone else is capable of living out their dreams is.

Ridding yourself these faceless barriers is not an easy task, but it can be done. Once you're able to release yourself from their grasp it becomes easier to keep them from interfering in your life again.

Casting Self-Doubt & the Fear of Failure Out of Your Life

Step 1: Acknowledge that self-doubt & the fear of failure are sabotaging you: Self-doubt and the fear of failure are powerful because we deny they exist. We don't want to believe that sometimes we're the only ones holding ourselves back. It's much easier for us to place blame on others. After we've run out of scapegoats we make up lame excuses to explain why we can't do this and that. When you acknowledge that you may be working against yourself you're able to start working for yourself.

Step 2: Write down what self-doubt & the fear of failure have kept you from doing: Whether it was applying for a job or taking one, write it down. Whether it was quitting your tear-producing job and starting that cool business you envisioned, or traveling the world instead of getting a job, write it down. Write down the plans you had for your career in college that you talked yourself out of when you graduated. You will be amazed at all the dreams you've abandoned while plagued with self-doubt and the fear of failure.

Step 3: Write down what your reasons were for not doing what you wanted: Right under each of your abandoned goals write down why you chose not to pursue them. The truth may be you didn't apply for a job you thought was perfect for you because you didn't think the employer would think you were perfect for the job. Perhaps you didn't accept a challenging position because you were afraid you couldn't meet the challenges. Maybe you never started your own business because you were afraid you'd look stupid if it failed. Write it all down. You may find that what once seemed like good reasons for your inaction now appears unimportant and silly. Now imagine what your career would be like had you done what your heart wanted. Imagine the path you'd be walking on. It's probably the one you wish you were walking on now.

Step 4: Begin speaking positive things into existence: You are smart, you are beautiful, you are creative, you are talented. You are worthy of a career twice as successful as you hope it will be, and it can be yours. What are you talking about? It *will* be yours! Start replacing the put-downs you feed yourself with words of encouragement and praise. Talk about what you can achieve and why you're capable of achieving that and more. If you're not feeling that, then you'll have to fake it until you make it. When you wake up in the morning thank God for not giving you a spirit of self-doubt or fear and then count your accomplishments one-by-one. After that, say aloud the goals you've made for your career and the qualities you have that will help you achieve them.

Step 5: Begin looking at opportunities in a new light: Once you've cut self-doubt and the fear of failure loose you may begin to see opportunities in a new light. What seemed risky may now appear exciting. What appeared too challenging may interest you now because you want to be challenged. You can now sift through all the plans you put in storage, or the garbage, and see which ones can still give your career the boost it needs. You'll find that the potential you have in your career and in life is enormous if you just take advantage of it.

Part 5
Banking in the Real World

Chapter 34

Real World Budgeting

*"I have enough money to last me the
rest of my life, unless I buy something."*
—Jackie Mason

Remember when your eyes lit up when you found out how much your salary was going to be? If not then you can play along. They told you $36,000 a year! You quickly divided that by 12 and got giddy thinking about what you could do on a $3,000 a month salary.

You could finally visit Hawaii and Jamaica, move into that beautiful apartment that had seemed above your means, afford a new car, get your hair and nails done every week, and even take your hard-working mom shopping once in a while. You had it all figured out, and what's more, you were going to have money to save!

But then reality hit you. You forgot about stingy Uncle Sam. You know he has to have his money. Okay, you thought—I can work with $2,300 a month. But then reality hit you again. You forgot about major bills, too. Then you sat down and calculated how much your rent, car note, insurance, utility bills, school loan payments and credit card bills totaled. That left $500 and some change. Okay, you said . . . I can still go to Hawaii when American Airlines has a special, get my car's windows tinted, have my hair and nails done once a month, and take mom shopping when there's a sale. But wait a minute! What about gas to get to the tint shop and beauty salon? What about spending money for the trip? And what about food and toilet paper?

Budgeting. It seems like the simplest task. Save some money here, put some money there, but budgeting is hard for most people because they think it's that simple. Budgeting takes time, effort and a heap of discipline. And if you're going to learn how to do it effectively, your best bet is to start now—not with next week's paycheck or next month's.

So go get a piece of paper, a trusty calculator and some tissues . . . in case you start to cry. Budgeting can be painful, too.

First you have to understand the reason why budgeting your money is so important. The main reason is that you can waste every hard-earned dollar you take home if you don't take control of your finances. Devising and sticking to a budget will also help you reach your monthly goal of paying all the bills, your short-term goal of having nice things, and your long-term goal of having peace of mind because you are financially secure and don't have to worry about money. Those are your goals aren't they?

For the most part, your money should be directed into the following categories:

1. Expenses: All the bills you have to pay, and things you must have to live and work: food, gas, toiletries, and miscellaneous items you have to pay for often.

2. Rainy Day Fund: Money is put into this category (normally into a savings account) for when your money isn't quite right. You'll use this if (God forbid) your transmission goes out, you must take the next flight out of town for an emergency, or if you lose your job for some reason. You never know what circumstance will have you digging in your pockets for a large amount of money. But you will be able to financially handle those rainy days that inevitably come if you prepare for them now. Experts recommend that you save an amount equal to three months of your living expenses.

3. Debt: Money in this category goes to all the people or companies you owe. We'll talk in more detail about this later.

4. Savings: Most financial advisers recommend saving at least 10 percent of your monthly income, although I encourage you to save much more—at least 15 percent. The money can be divided into two categories:

Short-term Savings: Money put into this category goes towards saving up for expenses you feel are important and desire in the near future, such as a trip, new car or wedding.

Long-term Savings: Money is put into this category so you can move out of your apartment one day, and live comfortably when you're no longer working.

Now get a notebook and sharpen a pencil—you're about to do your budget. Fill out the following on a separate sheet of paper as best as you can. First, determine how much you actually take home every month after Uncle Sam has robbed you—sorry—taken his fair share. If you get money from another source that comes regularly, such as a second job or child support, figure out that amount too. Now add both of those figures up. This is your total monthly income.

Next, estimate how much each of your monthly "must be paid" expenses are, using the list I have provided as a guide. Skip the expenses that you don't have and estimate how much the other expenses are. It's better to overestimate than underestimate how much you spend on expenses that vary each month, like electricity, gas and groceries. Once you've calculated all the expenses in this category, add them all up and deduct the figure from your total monthly income.

Sample Budget

1. Total Monthly Income
Salary per month (after taxes): $2,300

Monthly "Must Be Paid" Expenses

Rent/Mortgage:	$600
Utilities (water,electricity,gas):	$125
Car Payment:	$250
Gasoline:	$150
Car Insurance:	$125
Cell Phone:	$75
Community transit:	$0
Groceries:	$200
Health Insurance:	$0
Laundry:	$0
Other Insurance:	$0
Personal Hygiene:	$50
School Loan Payments	$100
Telephone:	$30
Total credit card payments:	$100

Total Monthly "Must Be Paid" Expenses= $1,805

Income *minus* Monthly "Must Be Paid" Expenses=$495

Now move on to the monthly "I could live without it" expenses. These expenses are the ones that keep many people from budgeting effectively and saving. Because they are expenses we pay for whenever we feel the need, we hardly ever keep up with how much we are spending/wasting on these things we could live without. Instead of just spending money frivolously on things you want, but don't need, you need to budget them into your budget. You must decide how much money you can afford to spend on clothes, renting movies and personal care to be within your budget and have money left over to save each month. So, if you decide that you will only spend $50 a month on clothes, then according to your budget you will have to wait two months to buy a $75 jacket. If you said you'd only spend $25 on movies and it's the middle of the month and you've already used up $24.99 and want to go see the hottest new movie—then according to your budget you'll have to get someone to pay for you or watch it later on video. You have to take your budget seriously. In order for you to stay consistent with your budget you'll have to be much more conscious of where your dollars are going.

One of the biggest expenses that is hard to keep up with falls under "miscellaneous"—film for your camera, money you have to chip in for a birthday party, speeding tickets. You never can tell what you will unexpectedly need or have to pay for on a monthly basis. Therefore you should have at least $40 under miscellaneous.

Once you've set aside money for each expense in the monthly "I could live without it" expenses category, calculate the total. Then deduct the total from your total monthly income and the total from your monthly "must be paid" expenses category.

Monthly "I Could Live Without It" Expenses

Beauty Salon:	$60
Books/music:	$20
Cable/TV:	$30
Clothes:	$50
Dry-cleaning:	$0
Eating Out:	$60
Internet Access:	$20
Other Entertainment:	$0
Miscellaneous:	$40
Movies:	$20
Nail Salon:	$0
Work Lunch:	$40

Total Monthly "I Could Live Without It" Expenses: $340

Total Monthly Income ($2,300) *minus* Total Monthly "Must Be Paid" Expenses ($1,805) *minus* Total Monthly "I Could Live Without It" Expenses ($340)=$155.

In this budget the person has $155 left over, which is less than 10 percent of their after tax income. This person might want to look into sharing an apartment to reduce the rent and utilities, and carpooling to work if possible. There are also items that could be reduced under "I could live without it" expenses.

How much money do you have left? If you don't have at least 10 percent, you need to go back and see if you gave yourself too much of an allowance for things you can do without or if you are really just living above your means.

Below are two expenses that drain many people's bank accounts, and a list of budgeting tips.

Money Drainers

Your Car: One of the first things many people do when they get a new or better paying job is run out and buy a new car. This usually means a higher car note than they had and more expensive insurance. Think wisely before opting to get a brand new car, especially one that you know is too expensive. The money you spend on a higher car note can go into your savings, towards paying off your debts, or toward investing in something that won't depreciate the moment you buy it.

Your Apartment: Your apartment rent is probably the largest expense you have each month, so doesn't it make sense to be economical when choosing an apartment? Shop around for the very best deal when looking for an apartment, and remember that an apartment is something you don't own. The extra money you spend to stay in a premier apartment could be saved to put money down on a premier house.

Money Savers

Instead of . . . going out to lunch everyday during your work break . . . *You could* . . . go to the grocery store and buy food to make salads, sandwiches or soups for the week. This will help you save money and lose weight.

Instead of . . . paying for cable . . . *You could* . . . cut it off and commit yourself to reading more.

Instead of . . . paying for gym memberships . . . *You could* . . . find some people to work out with outdoors or buy some workout videos.

Instead of . . . getting your hair done every week . . . *You could* . . . find a style that you can do yourself and limit your trips to the salon.

Instead of . . . paying for dry-cleaning each week on all of your clothes . . . *You could* . . . dry clean only those clothes that must be dry-cleaned.

Instead of . . . spending exorbitant amounts on your cell phone bill . . . *You could* . . . switch to a cheaper plan and really wait until 9 p.m. to talk.

Instead of . . . driving to work everyday . . . *You could* . . . car pool with employees who stay close to you or use public transportation.

My money waster has always been food because I love going out to eat. After graduating I struggled with making sure all my bills got paid in full each month, but still found a way to spend at least $50 a week at restaurants. When I moved to New York I made less money than I did after graduating but still spent at least $75 a week because I had more restaurants to choose from. I graduated in 2000 so I estimate that between 2000 and 2004, the year I left New York, I spent more than $2,500 on food that wasn't made in my kitchen. I am now trying to force myself to only eat out once every two weeks or when someone else is paying. I have also bought a couple of cookbooks.

Other Helpful Hints To Budgeting Effectively

One very time saving and effective way to keep up with your spending habits and expenses is to use a budgeting software program like Microsoft's Money. Budgeting programs like Money tell you when your bills are due, track all of your expenses by category, keep track of as many saving and checking accounts you have, create forecasts to help you determine how much money you can save, and will even help you create a budget to get out of debt. Don't let anyone tell you that you're cheap for creating and sticking to a budget. The same people who spend money carelessly and complain when you have to skip going out to eat will probably be the same ones asking you for money in the long run.

Other Helpful Hints To Saving Effectively

One of the best ways I have found to save cash is to have a set amount of money electronically taken out of your bank account each month and transferred into a savings account that pays interest. Currently, HSBC (www.hsbcusa.com) and ING Direct (www.ingdirect.com) both offer FDIC-insured savings accounts with at least a 4 percent annual percentage yield. You can sign up online and there is not a minimum deposit or monthly fee.

To start saving for retirement take advantage of your employer's 401(k) plan and/or open a Roth IRA (individual retirement account) online with an investment management company. Have the money you're saving for retirement electronically taken out each month and put into your retirement account. You can visit CNN's website, www.cnnmoney.com, or buy a personal finance book, such as Suze Orman's *The Money Book for the Young, Fabulous and Broke*, to learn more about how to choose the right IRA and to receive expert financial advice.

I found it nearly impossible to save money consistently until I opened an online savings account and Roth IRA. I foolishly depended on myself to transfer a set amount of money each month into a savings account. The problem was that the savings account was tied to my checking account. I ended up dipping into my savings account nearly every month or putting in less than what I was supposed to. A year after I started "saving" I had less than $2,000 in my savings account; I had planned to have $6,000.

Once I opened an online savings account and Roth IRA my money immediately began to grow. I had a set amount of money electronically transferred from my checking account to the new accounts every month on the same day I got paid. This way, when I looked at my checking account balance I never saw the money I was trying to save, and thus could not spend it. I check both accounts every other week to see how much more money I've earned and to give myself something to smile about.

Chapter 35

Reducing Your Post-College Debt

> *"Credit buying is much like being drunk.*
> *The buzz happens immediately, and it gives you a lift.*
> *The hangover comes the day after."*
> —Dr. Joyce Brothers

As college students many of us did some very curious things with our money that we pretended made sense. I convinced myself that putting new bedroom furniture on credit cards was okay because I'd be able to pay if off in full when I graduated. Going on little shopping sprees with Express and Foley's cards was okay too because I'd pay those bills off when I got my student loan refund. Now, I couldn't reasonably argue why asking for more money in student loans than I needed for tuition and bills made sense, but that didn't matter. I felt I'd have the rest of my life to pay it back.

Well, the rest of my life soon came. I nearly fainted when I received the first statement showing how much I owed the federal government. And that was before I went to grad school. If you're like me and most recent college graduates, you're pinching yourself for not listening closely to your financial aid advisers and for not reading those anti-credit card signs on campus. What's worse, you're getting bills in the mail that all say the same thing: It's payback time!

Being knee-deep in debt after graduation is not uncommon. According to the American Council on Education's latest findings, students who graduated from a public college or university owed an average of $16,928 in federal student loans. Students who graduated from private schools left owing an average of $17,125 to the government. And according to a study undertaken in 2004 by Nellie Mae, a top originator of postsecondary education loans, the average undergraduate carried a credit card balance of $2,169.

Basically, a lot of us owe a lot of people money. Yet, while it's often a struggle to pay all the bills fresh out of college, don't overlook the importance of getting started paying off the debt you've accumulated. It has to be done. Too much debt can eventually mean your lack of a car, house, important future loans, and wealth.

It's best to start reducing your debt as soon as you've got money coming in on a regular basis. If you're budgeting your money effectively then digging yourself out of debt will be much easier. The following are steps you can follow to pay off your existing credit card and school loan debt.

Digging Yourself Out Of Credit Card Debt

1. Determine how much credit card debt you're in: Gather up all your credit card statements and write down the balance of each card, the interest rate, and the minimum amount due each month.

2. Keep your two major credit cards with the lowest rates: Cut up the others and close their accounts immediately. Also cancel department store cards no matter how often you shop there. To stay out of debt you should purchase goodies with cash or your debit card.

3. Analyze your spending habits and see where you can cut costs: This goes back to budgeting. Think of all the things you waste money on and don't really need. Instead of spending $15 a month getting a fill-in, you could show off the beauty of your natural nails and add that $15 to the $10 you were going to send The Limited. Do you have to go out to eat twice a week? Isn't it time you learned to cook a real meal anyway? Why are you buying another pair of black heels?

4. Start paying off the card with the lowest balance and work your way up: Tackle the smallest balance first so paying off your credit card debt won't seem like such an impossible task. As shown in step 3, see where you can cut unnecessary expenses and then pay as much as you possibly can each month on the card with the lowest balance. It's okay to pay the minimum on the rest; however, paying as much as you can on the first card you've chosen to pay off is extremely important. There is no way you can beat credit card debt by paying just the minimum balance on all of your cards. Mailing off checks for $10 may seem sweet and simple, but you don't want to be 50 years old and still sending in that same amount on those very same cards.

For example, if you owe $2,750 on a credit card with an 18 percent interest rate, and you only pay the minimum monthly payment of $68.75 (2.5 percent of the balance), it will take you about 21 years (254 months) to pay it off. Your total payment for this credit card would be $6.490.66 because you will have paid $3,740.66 in interest, which is more than you initially borrowed. Scary, isn't it?

5. When you've paid one card off start paying off another: Use the same strategy with all of your cards. After you've paid off the card with the lowest balance, start paying off the next card with the lowest balance.

Digging Yourself Out Of Student Loan Debt

Paying off your school loans can be a little trickier than credit cards and a lot harder because of all the money you may owe. If you were like many undergraduates, once you got the bill each semester showing what you owed you looked at it once and filed it away. At the end of your final semester you received the total bill and almost cried.

The grace period the government and private lenders give you comes much faster than expected. But once it's over you must start paying what is rightfully theirs. The amount they ask for each month under a standard repayment plan can seem outrageously high, but it's the amount you need to pay to be finished before your children start college.

Under the federal government's standard repayment plan you repay your loan in equal monthly installments over a period of no longer than 10 years. This ensures a quick payoff and minimizes your total interest costs. If you can, find a way without borrowing money from someone else to pay the amount asked, and try to pay even more than that. If you can't, here are some of your options:

1. Extended Repayment: This plan stretches the loan repayment term between 12-30 years, depending on how much you borrowed. Payments are still fixed each month, but will be less than under a standard repayment plan. You'll pay more interest because the loan term is longer.

2. Graduated Repayment: This option is designed for borrowers whose salary starts out low, but is expected to increase over time. Payments start out lower and increase according to a set schedule. Interest payments will be higher than under a level repayment option. This plan requires you to prove your income to your lender.

4. Income Sensitive Repayment: This option also lets borrowers begin with low payments and progress to higher payments. Instead of increasing according to a set schedule, however, payments under this plan rise as the borrower's income rises. This plan also requires you to prove your income to a lender.

5. Direct Lending Income Contingent Repayment (ICR) Program: This plan is as tricky as its name. When you barely have enough money to buy ramen noodles, you can qualify for this plan. Your ICR payment is figured as a percentage of your monthly income. The lender tries to determine what you can reasonably afford to pay. The trouble with the ICR payment is that it may be even less than the monthly interest accruing on your loan. So, if you're supposed to be paying $200 a month ($140 for the principal and $60 for the interest) and you are only paying $40 a month, you would not be paying all of the interest, much less the principal amount. This plan can waste your money and keep your loan growing.

6. Deferment: A deferment is a temporary suspension of your monthly loan payment. If you have an unsubsidized loan your principal payments will be postponed, but interest will be charged and added to the principal balance of your loan. Principal payments are postponed and interest is not charged on subsidized loans. The lender will require proof that you qualify for deferment, which may be because you're in school at least half-time, are unemployed, are a working mother, or are in the armed forces.

7. Forbearance: A forbearance is also used to temporarily suspend or reduce your monthly school loan payments. Like a deferment, it may cost you dearly through the interest that's added onto the principal balance each month. You also have to qualify for a forbearance.

Lenders advise that you call them before the grace period is up to discuss your options. Please remember that not paying back your loans is not an option. Unlike a car or house, lenders can't repossess your education, but they can make it impossible for you to get a car or house by destroying your credit.

Part 6
Real World Stories

Yvonne Chase on Doing It Your Way

From the time I was a little girl I wanted to be Miss America. I also wanted to be a famous daytime TV soap opera star on none other than *All My Children*. I dreamt of singing, modeling and having my face plastered on the cover of *Essence* magazine. Of course, I would also be a top anchor on the six o'clock news. And I didn't want to do these things as hobbies when I had time; I planned to make my living doing *all* of these things.

I think I came out of my mother's womb talking with a microphone in my hand. I love to talk and can converse with anyone about anything at anytime. Turn the camera on and I come alive instantaneously. God gave me the personality and gifts that lend themselves easily to all the things that I wanted to do and be when I was younger. However, I grew up in a very strict Christian Caribbean home and wasn't exactly encouraged to use all the creative energy I had been blessed with.

My parents had a hard time wrapping their minds around me making a living as an entertainer. They had something a little bit more practical in mind. "How about being a school teacher or a nurse, doctor or lawyer? What about a career in computers or technology?" they asked. In their eyes, I wasn't "normal"—I was different. One day my father told me that I was the most different child he had and he wanted to know where I came from. My other siblings were considered normal because they all desired normal careers. I, on the other hand, had a strong creative gene that needed to be satisfied.

There were many rules in the Chase family, and attending a four-year-college was one of the biggest. And there were other rules attached to this big rule, including that you had to attend full-time and never take breaks between semesters.

By the time I was set to go to college, the constant questioning of my career goals had made me rethink my plans. I convinced myself that perhaps I should seek a "more practical" career, and I decided that I would become a gynecologist. So naturally, when I went to register at Brooklyn College I planned to enroll in medical classes and science courses, but all of those were filled. The only classes available were TV/radio production classes. I couldn't go home unregistered, so I went with the TV/radio production program, which soon became my major.

God had thrown me right back into the world of creativity. I loved it! My first internship was at a TV studio anchoring the news and being the weather girl. I was in heaven! Every summer I interned at radio and TV stations learning all that I could about my future career. I wasn't sure of exactly where I fit in but I sure was having a lot of fun finding out. I was a reporter for Brooklyn Cable News and I was out there reporting and covering the Democratic National Convention. I was thrilled to be able to say, "This is Yvonne Chase reporting live from 34th Street and 6th Avenue. Back to you Alex in the studio."

Graduation soon came. Armed with a college degree and lots of experience from the many internships I had at CNN, KISS-FM and other media outlets, I was ready to hit the ground running and find my first job in TV. It was tough finding a job in the media industry, I won't lie about that, but I networked and talked to everyone I met to see who knew who. At one point I became discouraged and thought about entering an easier field; my parents were still bugging me to do something else with my life. But something told me to not give up so easily.

One day I went back to KISS FM to talk with An Tripp, an on-air personality who had become a mentor to me. She didn't have the answers about how or where I could find a job, but she gave me a lead about a new talk show that would soon be airing. She didn't have a contact name or phone number, but she did know the name of the host and a network he had been a part of previously. That was all she had to tell me. I went home, dialed 411, got the phone number to that network and did what I do best—talk. A woman named Krystal Krews told me that Gordon Elliott, the man I needed to speak with, was going to be in the building the next day at 9 a.m. If I ever meet her I'm going to give her a big hug for talking to me, a total stranger, for 45 minutes.

She told me that Gordon Elliot was a very tall man with a heavy Australian accent. That was all I needed to know. I went to the library, got my resume right, went to Kinko's to have it printed on "good" paper, pulled out my Corporate Suzie suit and prepared myself to meet my new boss in the morning. The next day I got up nice and early, went to the gym, ate breakfast, got dressed and took the train to FOX Studios in Manhattan. I waited in the lobby like a stalker looking for a very tall man with a heavy Australian accent. It was nearing 10:30 a.m. and I hadn't see him, but my spirit told me to wait. I'm so glad I listened because I soon saw a man almost seven feet tall preparing to leave the building. I wasn't sure if it was him but there was only one way to find out. I went up to him, introduced myself, and asked if he was Gordon Elliott. He was! I gave him my resume and told him that I was a recent college graduate with a degree in TV production looking for a job. I let him know that I heard about his upcoming talk show and would love the opportunity to work on it and be a part of his staff. By the time I got home there was a message on my voicemail from his office calling to schedule an appointment. My interview was later that week and I started my first job in TV as a production assistant on the *Gordon Elliott Show*.

After that blessed break I moved from show to show for two years until I reached the level of producer. Was it easy? Heck no! It was the equivalent of swimming with sharks and fighting with wolves all day but I loved my work. I loved writing scripts. I loved pre-interviewing potential guests and learning the details of their story. And I loved collaborating with the director and hosts to put on a great show. But what I loved the most were all the free books I got to take home from the many authors that sent them in. I love to read and that is how I built my home library. My parents hated to see me stressed out, working 17-hour days and on weekends while not having a stable gig. Most of TV production is freelance work, especially on start-up/new shows. You get paid well but you don't get benefits and you work like a one-armed slave. "If only you would get a stable job with benefits" were words I heard from my parents repeatedly. However, I remained focused on creating the career I envisioned.

In 1996, I took a big step and moved to Los Angeles, the entertainment capital of the world. I thought that living in LA would better allow me to see what the world of TV was all about, after all, that is where TV was created and developed. My executive producer at the *Gordon Elliott Show* told me, "One day you are going to become a big time producer and I can't wait to tell your story." I moved to Los Angeles to create that story.

My parents thought I had lost my natural mind. They were 100 percent non-supportive of my decision and they let me know it in word and deed. My mother didn't even get up to see me off to the airport on March 22, 1996. None of my siblings understood this move. I didn't know anyone in LA, had no place to live and had no job, but what I did have was a whole lot of faith. Matthew 17:20 says: "If you have faith as small as a mustard seed, you can say to this mountain, 'Move from here to there,' and it will move. Nothing will be impossible for you." I kept those words in my heart, $6,000 in my pocket, and six bags that looked like I was transporting dead bodies to JFK Airport and boarded an 8 a.m. flight to my new life.

Within one week I had the essentials to start my new life in La-La Land: a job, a car, and a place to stay. How was I able to do all of that so fast? When God guides, he always provides. My friend Michelle in New York had a friend of a friend of a friend who was starting a business and needed an assistant. I became that assistant. Michelle had another friend, Duane, who had a two-bedroom apartment with an extra room to spare. That is where I lay my head until I moved into my own place. Duane had a mechanic who had an old car that looked good and ran great in the back of his shop. That was my first car. Faith in God, courage, boldness and talking with confidence took me a long way in LA and in life. But despite my initial success, I found that living in Los Angeles was not easy; it was very brutal and extremely competitive—even more so than New York. I got a rude awakening, but I temped and did freelance production work to keep myself afloat.

I haven't had the opportunity to run for Miss America, but I sure have been Ms. Bahamas in local pageants. My face hasn't been plastered on the cover of *Essence*, but I sure have had an article published in the magazine, along with my photo. I haven't reached super model status like Naomi Campbell or Tyra Banks, but I have done my share of modeling and fashion shows. I've even been on TV and in movies. And I haven't won that daytime Emmy or Grammy yet for my gospel album, but as long as I'm alive I know it's all still very possible.

One thing I know for sure is this: when you do what you love, the money will come and the peace of mind will always be present. It won't always be easy, but at the end of the day you have to follow your heart. Not long ago I was listening to *My Way* by Frank Sinatra and tears began to roll down my face.

I've lived a life that's full
I've traveled each and every highway
And more, much more than this
I did it my way
Yes, there were times, I'm sure you knew
When I bit off more than I could chew
But through it all, when there was doubt
I ate it up and spit it out
I faced it all and I stood tall
And did it my way

Today, I am living in Los Angeles and working hard to ensure that my star continues to shine bright. My move to LA helped me develop more than just my career; it gave me my calling and my purpose in life: to empower single women to live their life to the fullest. My #1 mission is to create a movement of available and happy single women that enter relationships out of want and not need. I plan to use my background in TV production to bring my message to a TV or radio station near you.

Are there days when I wish I was a school teacher or in some other profession working in a stable environment, bringing home a steady paycheck? Absolutely! But that is not the script that was written for my life. I've learned the hard way that when you deviate from your pre-written script, life becomes very difficult, challenging and unhappy. And even though your choices or your life may not make sense to well-meaning family members, you still have to do what works for you. You have to do it your way.

Yvonne Chase is a dating coach, writer, speaker and daytime talk show producer. Visit her website www.availableandhappy.com.

Jean Thompson on Getting Out of a Rut

I've always been told that the ticket to career advancement and higher earning power is a master's degree. My experience has confirmed this to be true in many fields. It is not, however, the only way to get ahead. There's another way, and I stumbled upon it quite unexpectedly. I call it "earning a master's degree on the street."

After toiling as a metropolitan newspaper reporter and editor for about six years, I suddenly woke up feeling restless—bored, actually. Others might think that reporting is endlessly exciting. While it is true that every story presents a new challenge, the process of newsgathering and writing can begin to feel routine.

My performance reviews were adequate, my work record clean. I was not the office wizard or prize-winner, but I was a solid workhorse on whom editors could rely to keep the pages filled. That's good enough for lots of people, yet in time I realized it was not good enough for me. I wanted a greater role in decisions that shaped the daily newspaper and public opinion. How to escape this rut?

One answer might be to enroll in a master's program. Unfortunately, with a mortgage and family-planning issues looming, graduate school teased me from just out of reach. Perhaps I could attend one or two classes on weekends or evenings, just to recharge my battery, I thought. But which classes would benefit me most? I felt trapped.

Meanwhile, I became increasingly resentful as I watched people with less seniority advance to more interesting and better paying assignments. During a phone call with a friend who had a job in upper management, I groused, "What do they know that I don't?" "Find out," she demanded, putting me on the spot.

That was the day my fortunes turned: my first day of "school." Now, I'll admit, in the beginning I wasn't just startled by my friend's prodding, I was miffed. I interpreted that challenge as a dare, or worse, an accusation.

She was forcing me to look within, to honestly assess what I knew, who I knew and what I knew how to do. I might have to approach people who had leapfrogged over me, or the bosses who promoted them, to get the answers to my questions. Damn!

I dawdled a while but the next time we talked my friend asked again if I had found out what key information I was missing. Finally, looking at myself in the mirror, I asked myself what I was waiting for. How would a reporter handle this assignment if she were writing a story about getting ahead? Who would she interview? What questions would she ask?

Before long, I had a mental list, and soon, a notebook full of questions that I wanted answered: What are the major attributes of leaders in my company? Where did they go to school? What classes helped them most? What would they study today if they could? To whom do they turn when they get stumped? (They're only human, I figured.) What do I have to learn and who do I have to know in the organization? Do they belong to certain clubs or professional societies? What do they read? How do they keep learning?

I made a short list of people in the company who seemed approachable (and a few who absolutely terrified me but who seemed always to be at the center of major happenings). I put some of my ambitious peers on the list, and some of the rising stars. One was a high-ranking manager who had always claimed to practice an open-door policy; I decided to call his bluff. And I put my own boss on the list, out of respect, because I knew that she'd get wind of it when I started quizzing people up the ladder from her.

It took me a while to summon the courage to start interviewing. I know that sounds strange coming from a reporter, but this wasn't any old story. First, I had to get my emotions in the right place. I had to be ready to hear whatever critique of my skills and performance might be dished out. Don't ask a question if you're afraid of the answer.

And so it began. Some people had little to say. Some gave me insights on the company that I never expected to hear. Remarkably, almost everyone I approached was flattered to be asked for advice. They enjoyed talking about themselves and their achievements. A few were snippy, and one blew me off. I guess they felt I was asking for some secret recipe.

My boss was surprised and a little suspicious, but ultimately encouraging. She told me that she had noticed my weeks-long depression and had not known how to motivate me. Once I identified for her what was wrong, she was able to give me suggestions on how to put some bounce back in my productivity.

In all, this informal interviewing took about a week (I deliberately tried to get it over with so it would not look like some type of campaign or malingering). Some chats were after hours, some during quick coffee breaks. A few of the interviews with executives required appointments.

I followed up with quick thank-you notes and then sat down alone in a favorite restaurant with my brimming notebooks. I soon discovered that people who advanced in my company had several traits in common:

- They were readers. Voracious readers. Some methodically read two to five newspapers a day, dissecting and comparing as they went. Many enjoyed fiction, but most consumed nonfiction, especially those who saw themselves as becoming experts in a given subject. Acquiring expertise in some body of knowledge mattered, and it didn't seem to matter what the subject was so much as how deeply the person came to know and understand it. No matter what field they were interested in, they all followed business news—on TV or on the internet or in the *Wall Street Journal.* That's where they learned who was winning and who was losing in many industries. That's where they looked for signs of economic trouble or relief that might inform our company's strategy, and trends on which we might capitalize. One more thing these readers had in common: they went for quality, not quantity. "Life is too short to read crap," one told me. After that, I asked each contact to name a single book about journalism that I absolutely should read.

• They respected workhorses but they revered mavericks. Risk-takers came in several stripes, from the loose cannons to the calculating chess players. The methodical and smart ones took well-planned risks and moved ahead (sometimes, the nuts did, too). But the bottom line was this: nobody got ahead by keeping his head down.

• They learned on the job from each other. If somebody got a great scoop, they'd clap him on the back and then, that night, buy him a beer and make him tell how he got it. There would be a lot of bluster and swagger too, but that's where a lot of learning and exchanging of techniques and advice took place. My head was swimming. I'd been skipping the after-work parties and these "events" because I felt self-conscious at them. How would I fit in as a sober black woman in a room full of beer-swilling, guffawing white big shots? I wasn't a teetotaler, and I actually don't mind ale, but I was trained by my Southern-born mama that this was a potentially bad-news scene. Suddenly, I realized that I had been missing out on the fraternal exchange of education.

• Some people got ahead by looking for, and then acing, specific types of assignments that demonstrated their mastery of levels of skill or specific techniques. Think like a student of martial arts: master a level, earn a belt, move ahead. Others got ahead by what I called "upwardly mobile thinking." You've heard this before: You want to get to management, dress like a manager. Well, the suit is nice, sister, but the brain is even more effective. If you're a lowly writer who wants to be an editor, think like an editor. If you're a sales clerk and you want to be the supervisor, study the supervisors, learn the lingo of inventory and price points, and find out how your corner of the business fits into the whole universe of your company. Read some of that stuff the company mails home if you've been treating it like junk mail, especially if you're a stockholder. You should also read proxy papers and other fine print. You'll be shocked what information they sometimes contain about your company, and your bosses and their salaries and bonuses. If you're in the front office, learn what's going on back in the boardroom where the decisions are made. The brain goes first, then the skills and work habits follow.

* Nobody who moved ahead waited for permission. If no one is handing you growth-potential assignments on a platter, go out and make them for yourself, one source said. You don't have to be terribly obvious or public about it. Just discreetly assign yourself the task or the challenge and get it done. If your boss is sincere about helping you grow, she'll show you the way. If she's not (and some are not), you can still imbed your personal growth challenge somewhere within a project that your boss has assigned, and reap the reward. Or make it part of a volunteer project. Find a mentor—someone in higher management or someone who has done your job before—to talk to about the skills and techniques that you are trying to master, so you can be sure you're going in the right direction and so you'll get a pat on the back for it. Remember, you need no one's permission to grow.

I distilled all of this into a personal action plan: my master's degree on the street. It was very simple, mapped out in ink in my day planner over a one-year period:

♦ A list of must-read books, with a goal of reading one a month.

♦ A list of skills and techniques that I wanted to study and master, with a goal of "demonstrating" my mastery once a month. If my boss could not give me an assignment that involved my particular skill-of-the-month, I would dig up a story on my own that would give me the opportunity. I'd tell myself, "This one's for my master's degree," and just go for it. (Surprise of all surprises, each one of these stories did run, and soon enough, colleagues were asking me, "So, how did you get that scoop?")

♦ I identified a couple of small groups of colleagues who did more than grumble when they got together. They talked shop and ideas and techniques, and I made it a point to hang out with them every now and then so I could listen.

♦ The big boss with the open door had been very giving with advice, so I went back to him and presented my crazy idea. This is my "master's degree," I told him, and I hope you'll oversee my education. All I'm asking for is a chat with you once a month to talk about my goal for that month, and how I will study it and demonstrate it. At first, he laughed (okay, I figured, I've got his attention), but he could see that I was serious. I showed him the reading list, and asked him for more titles. We agreed to talk again in a month.

My career was never the same after that. Each month I had a goal that was my very own. My boss noticed my newfound energy and began tossing better stories my way. My mentor rewarded me with praise, introduced me to his colleagues who shared their knowledge and connections, and arranged for other incentives for me.

I knew I had cracked the code when I was at a company party (yes, I learned how to navigate these, usually with a glass of soda or plain water in my hand). I noticed the beer crowd gathered around a bar, telling war stories. I saw my mentor in the thick of them, so I sidled over.

"C'mon, Jean, let me buy you a drink," he said, inviting me into the group. I froze for a moment, and then I stammered something like, "I'm not much of a drinker. I probably only drink one beer a year."

"Whoa, that makes this a special occasion," somebody said. "If you only drink one beer a year, then surely we would be flattered if you would choose to drink it with us."

After that, the "beer of the year" became a long-running joke between me and my colleagues, one that symbolically broke down a divide between our culturally different and not-so-different worlds. It gave us a way to connect, and after that I never felt pressured to order anything at company affairs. I had set a boundary without making anybody feel uncomfortable (including myself).

That year, I earned my "degree" and many accolades. Within a year, I also earned a promotion that in time led to the top ranks of management.

I plan to return to college eventually, to earn the official piece of paper. It's helpful for anyone who wishes to teach at the college level. Meanwhile, I truly can say that I've been blessed with great mentors and colleagues who helped me learn how to get out of a rut, and how to get ahead in business by setting and meeting personal growth goals. You can do it too by earning "a master's degree on the street."

Jean E. Thompson is a former associate editor of the editorial pages at The Baltimore Sun newspaper. Currently, she is internship coordinator for Black College Wire, a nonprofit news service that trains student journalists from historically black colleges and universities. She has a bachelor's degree in communication studies from the University of Southern California.

Talia Nye-Keif
on Checking Your Problems at the Door

I once had a dear friend who I worked with in El Paso, Texas. He was several years older than I, had been in the business a lot longer than I had, and was someone for whom I had a great deal of respect. He gave me several nuggets of wisdom during the years we worked together, but one of them has always stayed with me.

I occasionally was in the habit of letting my personal emotions surface at work. "How's it going, T?" they'd ask. "Oh, okay, but I have a headache," I'd say. Other responses were "My boyfriend and I are fighting," or "My mother is driving me nuts," or "I can't stand this outfit I have on..." You get the picture. I truly wasn't in a bad mood, nor was I at the point of needing crisis intervention. My flip answers were my way of humanizing myself, trying to make myself seem more like a "regular human being." Unfortunately, I was being perceived as a whining, self-indulgent priss who never felt good about herself.

What I learned was that folks at work don't really want to hear about your personal life; they all have problems of their own. So, my friend's advice to me, advice I am happy to pass along, is to take a deep breath at the front door before you enter your place of work. Free your mind of whatever troubles you've left at home, put on your "work face" and wear it with a smile! I know it sounds a little hokey, but this tactic has worked for me for the past 15 years. Often I must consciously work to lose the attitude or the depression or the anger or the anxiety or the stress that hitched a ride with me to work that morning. Hanging on to the handle of the door that leads to my office, I'll take a few cleansing breaths and tell myself, "Okay, time to focus. I'm at work now and I have a reputation to protect, a job to do, a career to advance," or words to that effect.

Your phrase will be different from mine. We're different people, and we have different problems. But remember, we all have problems and we all have to check them at the door.

Talia Nye-Keif is a former U.S. Air Force sergeant, television news journalist, and public relations professional. She presently is attending St. Mary's University School of Law and plans to pursue a career of legal and political advocacy. Talia lives in San Antonio, Texas, and is the mother of two lovely daughters and wife of a police detective.

Angelene Hall on the Loss of Camaraderie Among African-Americans in the Professional Workplace

Not very long ago, my friend and I sat in the new university bistro lamenting the isolation we feel on a campus that has more African-Americans and other ethnic groups now than it has had in its 132-year history. We reflected on the time, the seventies, when faculty and staff organizations were created to address discrimination in hiring and retention, organizations which became even more critical during the Reagan era. Not only did these groups help to fight our racial battles, they also gave us an opportunity to come together and share information. More than that, these activist groups provided a forum for African-Americans to become acquainted and experience a sense of belonging. However, since many of those who were instrumental in the development of these organizations have retired and/or been replaced by younger faculty with a different political orientation, the camaraderie died a quick death and gave birth to a group who cut the umbilical cord of race consciousness before the ink dried on the forms of the retirees.

We sat in the bright new building, our eyes wandering from one area to another, cognizant of the modest difference the university's quest for diversity had made over the years. There were dark faces among us. The problem was, however, we couldn't seem to make eye contact. There was not that codified understanding of, "We're here in this strange place, but we're here together," nor the nod of consciousness and common history. It was all gone and in its place was an innocuous dismissal of any racial connection, suggesting there is no kinship here.

In one of my futile efforts to make contact, for example, I noticed a black female standing at the pop machine, waiting for water to become coke, and I decided to approach her. I could tell she was a colleague because she wore her identification badge clamped just above the very detailed pockets of her navy blue suit. Pretending I wanted a refill, I eased up to the machine and said, "You'd think with these prices, we wouldn't have a problem with coke machines." Chuckling, I raised my glass and introduced myself. Without turning her head from the pop fountain, the woman glanced at me out of the corners of her eyes, made a noncommittal "hmm," and walked away.

The woman's reaction is more common than not in the professional world. How many times have we found ourselves in a predominantly white setting and looked around to those one or two other dark faces only to be met with a look that implied, "Don't even think about moving in this direction." Already the "outsider within," we worry about what white folks will think if they see more than one of us at a time, especially if we are together. The distance and isolation that many African-Americans sense from one another are probably the result of years of implied and stated indoctrination that said the goal of the black professional should be assimilation to the extent of racial invisibility.

The fear and loathing commonly typical of our professional relationships are, ironically, loaded guns pointed directly at us. Our marginal positions in many of these professional settings have come with years of struggle for not only inclusion, but full participation and appropriate recognition of our skills and talents. Now that we have made some inroads into the academy and the corporate world, why not use whatever clout we have to advance the professional lives of the group as a whole? Our reluctance to associate and work directly with each other is detrimental to both our individual and group success.

For example, we do not always have people to critique our work objectively, give us the proper feedback, or just say, "I've got your back." And because we are keenly aware of our isolation, we sometimes try to pretend we do not need anyone's guidance. We believe we can make it on our own; we can survive without anyone giving us suggestions that might steer us in the most propitious direction. When one of us has information or skills that could help another in career elevation, our attitude towards who we are often precludes such assistance, ergo, another lost opportunity for all involved.

What this means, of course, is that too often there is no one to look out for our interests because of the fear of association or being considered a part of "that group." Moreover, our efforts to avoid each other and certainly our fears of being identified as "one of those black people," prohibit our acquiring the benefits of sharing information and therefore creating opportunities for each other's advancement. It is similar to the black politician who runs for office on the platform of *not* running as a black politician, but a politician for all the people. With this type of racial detachment, many of us have no sense of connection in the professional world or elsewhere and ultimately end up asking, "Where is my place?" or "Where do I belong?"

So what is the solution to this dilemma? How do we create a professional environment conducive to the prosperity and sense of belonging for all of us? The answer begins with overcoming black self-hatred. Some of my students have tried to explain away self-hatred by arguing that it results from centuries of black repression. However, this repression has been met with both individual and group acts of resistance. These acts of resistance, whether exemplified by an individual who defied existing stereotypes, or by groups who actively engaged in the struggle for equal rights, represented a people who believed in themselves, demanded equal treatment, and had enough self-love to realize they deserved equal access to the blessings of this country. The struggle for Civil Rights, for example, was not simply a move by a group of people to fit into the American mainstream. It was the realization of a people's worth, an affirmation of selfhood, and ultimately a testimony of self-love.

With self-hatred no longer an obstruction to prosperity in the workplace, African-Americans can now see each other as resources in the professional world. We can rely on each other and develop networks. This time African-Americans can come together and create forums for providing information, generating new ideas, and helping each other to develop professionally. We have tried everything else to garner that elusive success that the system suggests we can acquire if only we work hard enough and of course, know the right people. Our assumption has been that the right people ostensibly meant white people. We have integrated, assimilated, became our own enemies and none of these have worked in our favor. The one thing we have not tried during these so-called days of diversity is coming together as African-Americans in our respective arenas.

Changing our attitudes towards ourselves as African-Americans will help us to deal with the intellectual and cultural isolation, aloneness and lack of place so characteristic of our current professional life. Our working together, serving as mentors and providing support systems for each other are what we need to prosper as a group in the world we fought to penetrate. These are the qualities we used when we were all we had. I am not suggesting a return to the days where struggle typified our entire world, but rather that we look at our past and extract from it the sense of collective well-being, good will, and professional prosperity.

Dr. Angelene Jamison-Hall is a professor of African-American Studies and Women Studies at the University of Cincinnati. She is a graduate of Bennett College for Women, (B. A. in English), the University of Cincinnati (M. A. in English), and the Union Graduate School (Ph.D. in African-American Studies). Her scholarship appears in such collections as World Literature Criticism, 1500 to the Present; Censored Books: Critical Viewpoints; Sage: A Scholarly Journal of Black Women, the Western Journal of Black Studies, and the Journal of Negro Education.

Vickie Stokes on Expecting the Unexpected

I've learned over the years that you must trust God to deliver the things you have been asking for, and to expect the unexpected because you never know when He will choose to bless you nor who He will choose to use to answer your prayer. He's certainly shown me that He works in mysterious ways.

I already had a job in Dallas, Texas with a wonderful company, and had been there for eight years working faithfully, but the time was coming for me to move on and spread my wings. I researched many companies because I wanted to be at a place that was stable, flexible with work hours, and capable of compensating their employees fully (i.e. tuition reimbursement, 401(k), travel, etc). After surfing the net tirelessly, reading the newspaper day in and day out and going back and forth to the library, I discovered this jewel of a company. They were a multi-billion dollar technology company with a name and reputation that surpassed the competition and they had positions and offices in many states, so advancement and relocation was on the horizon for me.

I could see myself sitting behind my new cherry wood desk, ordering my new business cards and nameplate and setting up my voicemail message. I could not believe I had found my dream job!! There was, however, one small problem: they recruited only five times a year, mostly on college campuses, and when they held their job fair locally it was by invitation only. In other words, I had to know someone already at this incredible company who could put my name on the invitation list. Well, I didn't have a connection on the inside, but I was not going to let that stop me because I was determined to get hired by this company. I prayed and prayed, seeking an answer to my dilemma. I finally decided to just fax my resume as many times as it took to get a call back. They had asked candidates not to fax resumes, but they left me with no choice. I faxed my resume once, twice, 25, 62 times. I know the people in the human resources department got tired of seeing my resume come across their fax machine, but I figured sooner or later they would have to respond. Well, after two years I still hadn't received a response. I guessed I was just another piece of paper to them. I was losing hope fast and the fight was turning into defeat. But just when I was going down for the third count God decided to show up in my situation and use an unlikely source to bless me with my dream job.

After two years of faxing my resume to human resources, I discovered that I had a connection the whole time on the inside. It wasn't just a connection, but a bona fide hook-up because a family member (yes, I said a family member) was already working for this company. She called me one day out of the blue and asked if I was still interested in working there.

I wondered how she knew I was interested. I didn't remember telling her about my endeavor. Besides, I didn't think I was big on her list. She was married into my family and wasn't a big hit with us back in the day. So I guess I just totally blocked it out of my mind that she worked for this company. Or perhaps my pride kept me from asking her for help.

Well, after two years of faxing my resume and drowning in my sorrows, this person was coming to the rescue. Again, you never know when God is going to bless you or whom He will use to deliver the blessing. My grandmother used to say in a prayer, "Anyway you bless me Lord is okay with me." I understand what she meant now. I needed the help.

That family member was asked for a name of a person that was interested in working for this company. Out of all the people that had asked her for help over the years and who had helped her, she wanted to submit my name. Of course, I said

"YES" and the rest is history. I went on several interviews and my dream company made me an offer I couldn't refuse. I was finally in and ordering my business cards, name plates, and setting up my voicemail while sitting behind my cherry wood desk. I had a great boss, great pay, an expense account, etc. It was everything that I thought it would be.

I know now that the way it happened was all in God's plan and His timing. And I learned two more valuable lessons as I went through this process. First, if you believe strongly in something you have to wait until it manifests itself. You can't give up and you can't lose faith. Second, you can't mistreat and mishandle people. The person you act coldly towards today could be the same person interviewing you for a job tomorrow. I was given the chance to live one of my dreams, and even though I have since moved on from the company I am thankful for the process I had to go through to get me there.

Mrs. Vickie Stokes is the founder of Paradise Ministries, a non-profit that provides professional and spiritual growth workshops for battered women. She is married to Clausell Stokes, the CEO and president of S & S Counseling, a substance abuse facility for men and women. They have three beautiful children.

Regina Burns on
Chasing Away Those Pink Slip Blues

So, you're among the thousands of folks recently unemployed due to job cuts or whatever. It's scary, isn't it? Do you feel like a hole has opened up and swallowed you? That's how I felt in 1996 when the Memphis ad agency I did promotions and community relations work for gave me the ax.

Looking back, I'm grateful because I learned I could survive and could create a new way to earn a living. I hired myself. True, there have been good days and bad days that come with self-employment or any other aspect of life. But overall, I can honestly say that my new life has been good.

There have been some times when I had to wrestle with MMD "major money drama." But I did it and I learned a lot in the process. Now it's my turn to share some of what I've learned. Perhaps I can bring a smile to your lips and hope to your heart. After all, as comedian Steve Harvey says, "A laugh is a terrible thing to waste."

I've got a few offbeat, semi-zany, low-cost or no-cost suggestions that you may find helpful:

1. Read anything you can by Iyanla Vanzant. Who is Iyanla (E-yawn-la) Vanzant? Iyanla is a natural-born comedian and if she can survive, so can we. She wrote numerous bestsellers including *Acts of Faith*, and hosted her own talk show. Her autobiography, *Interiors*, is truly a page-turner.

2. Go the museum. Find out when museums in your area have free days and go. Learn about another culture or see some great art. When you get back to making your follow up calls you'll be in great spirits.

3. Get a book on tape from the public library and go walking. Audio books are available at most libraries free of charge and walking will do you good. Try this early in the morning for about 30 minutes and see what a difference it makes.

4. Find a support group or start your own. No need to bear your unemployed status alone. Get with some other folks and talk it out at least once a week. Consider setting up a telephone chain if need be or exchange email addresses.

5. Color. As in grab some crayons and a coloring book and color. Remember how good you felt in school when you colored in your coloring book? It's a creative process that you may not have used in awhile. It helps you relax and have fun at the same time.

6. Throw a party. That's right. Do the unexpected and have fun in the process. Invite your friends, neighbors and family and party down. While you're getting your groove on, you're letting people know that you're not dead, just unemployed, and life is still good. You can tell people how they can be of help, what you need, etc. Most people want to help you but need direction.

7. Write it all down. Keep a journal and write down all that stuff that's eating you up. Jot down all those words you wanted to say when they canned you, but didn't. Whatever is happening in your world, write it down.

Remember, just because you don't have a job doesn't mean your life is over. Sure, you have to make some adjustments. And maybe the way things happened was unfair. Once you get past the initial shock, go ahead and start grieving. Process the anger, hurt, disappointment, fear and depression. Then move on. I sent my former boss a thank you note the next week after I was downsized. I'd had a great experience but it was time for me to fly. Maybe this job loss thing is your time to rediscover you and to be replanted in a larger, roomier pot. It's up to you to determine whether you create the pot or locate a pot that's awaiting you.

Are you still breathing? Are you feeding yourself? Is your mind still working? Are you living indoors with running water? You are blessed!

Regina L. Burns is a Dallas-based writer, motivational speaker and community relations specialist with Harvest Reapers Communications Visit her website: http://www.harvestreapers.com.

Darcelle Whitaker on Working in Corporate America

I attended a historically black college, Florida A&M University, and received a degree in computer information systems. I graduated feeling that the world was mine to conquer for I was armed with a degree from a highly regarded university and I had a marketable skill set. But it took me more than 10 years to realize that that was not enough, and to understand that I must "own the keys" to the store in order to have a voice and be in complete control.

Florida A&M had an outstanding placement program. Recruiters from IBM, General Motors, Kodak, Shell Oil Company, Texaco, Mobil and a number of others frequented our campus, seeking top performers. Most important, I graduated during an era when affirmative action was strong, and this played an integral role in my landing my dream job at a Fortune 500 company. Unfortunately, neither predominately black or white colleges ever prepare African-Americans on how to survive in corporate America.

It is unwise and career debilitating to think that all one has to do is work hard and you will be justly recognized and rewarded. It is even more unwise to believe that you are measured against the same criteria as your white counterparts, even if the criteria is the standard performance measurement criteria used to rate and rank you amongst your peers. I found you must work two times harder, arrive much earlier, and leave even later than

your white counterparts. Your success is based on:
- Who you know at the top of the management chain.
- How well they like you.
- Networking only with the "right" people.
- Understanding the culture of the organization and most importantly never going against the culture.
- Conforming to the dress code.
- Communicating in a manner that mirrors your peers.
- Not using slang or "Ebonics."

I've found most corporate environments subconsciously invoke the "be seen and not heard" or "speak when spoken to" guideline. If you are an innovative visionary, be sure to choose a corporate culture that will embrace your contributions and provide an environment for growth.

I also advise you to take on tasks that will give you visibility, and to communicate with your supervisor daily and his boss at least twice a week. Also complete all tasks on schedule, and take on community projects sponsored by your corporation.

The most important advice is to mix and mingle with those who have visible roles. You must participate in or understand the "political game" and play it. Watch your back and do not participate in office gossip. It will come back to haunt you.

Something else I learned is to guard your ideas like you are in Fort Knox! Put all ideas in writing and present them in a forum. Never tell a peer your idea, for if it is a good idea, it will more than likely be presented as their own to your supervisor prior to a meeting. Follow up on all meetings and discussions with written documentation.

For your growth, take on all training classes that pertain to your assignment. Keep your resume updated. Write your short-term and long-term goals out and reference them often. Ensure your game plan is centered on these goals. Always network your skill sets and seek other opportunities. Learn as much as you can about your assignment. Be the resident "expert." Try to move around in the company frequently, every year or two.

I've learned a lot about corporate America and people in general from my experiences. I've also learned a lot about myself. If you find that corporate America is where you must work to pursue your dreams, then I wish you the best of luck!

Darcelle Whitaker is a graduate of Florida A&M University.

Francina Harrison on Deciding Who You Are Before Deciding What You Will Do

Since August 2003, our economy has witnessed severe layoffs, plant closings and overseas relocations for white and blue collar jobs. As a college graduate you may be wondering, "In this depressed labor market, is it possible to have the "American Dream" and be successful in the workforce and in life?" Absolutely! The proof is in the person. Look at Oprah, Bill Gates, Denzel, Beyonce, Tavis Smiley, and Sam Walton. They've found the way. In a nutshell, they focused on their potential, not the economic indicators. Successful people discovered who they were before they decided what they would do. It's deeper than a job with these folks. It's about delivering their passion, purpose, personality, and potential.

I'm convinced that the individuals listed above no longer have to go to work everyday. They work hard, but their careers have become another dimension of their personalities pushed beyond the "average" functioning levels. Successful people consistently strive to produce at 100 percent utilizing a true blend of purpose and occupation. But what about the rest of us? Can we attain that level of synergy in our professional career and life? Of course we can. However, understand that success does not come without cost. We must make a personal commitment to explore ourselves at deeper levels than we ever imagined. We must develop the authentic desire to uncover our wants and needs, in order to let go of old habits and gain new experiences. I challenge you to find out who you are before deciding what you'll do.

I learned the following seven steps to self-discovery as I tacked the real world after graduating from Norkfolk State University in 1997 with a master's in social work. I hope the seven steps help you discover who you are in work and in life.

1. Accept Who You Are: The ability to be comfortable in your own skin, and to find your own niche, is a must for today's competitive world. There is no one on this planet just like you. Learn to embrace and accept your originality, your body composition, the hue of your complexion, your voice, your essence, and your professional style. Once you have accepted "who you are," you can begin to share "what you bring" to the workforce, relationships, and the world. Your unique "brand" is a selling point that you must deliver in all of your networking experiences. Be the pacesetter who drives class and style. Set your standards and leave the crowd behind. Power Statement: Failure Happens When You Try To Become Something You Are Not.

2. Tap into Your Gifts and Talents: If you don't like something, you won't do it very well. In order to find your "fit" with a particular employer, you need to explore your interests, desires, natural gifts and acquired talents. Consider the following questions and write your responses. In what areas of your life have you received compliments with minimal efforts? What do you enjoy? What relaxes you? What would you do for free? How do you feel when you are doing that activity? Do you "dream out loud?" How would you describe your ideal environment? If all of your debts were paid, and you could do anything in the world, what would you be? Your answers may open the door for you to discover the best fit for your personality in the work environment. For instance, I enjoy helping people discover themselves. I need flexible, relaxed environments, open spaces, vibrant colors, limited supervision, and the ability to "go with it." I would not be successful working in the Patent and Copyright Office for the federal government (even if it's a GS-12 position); there are too many limitations. The result of an improper fit is friction, in which case poor performance and/or termination would likely follow. Power Statement: In The World of Success or Failure, Your Fit Makes The Difference.

3. Discover Your Strengths/Know Your Limitations: You can't sell what you don't know. Let's uncover your power. Consider the following examples to start your strength building process. Are you comfortable speaking in front of groups, keen with numbers, academically solid, business savvy, or an excellent leader? Don't discount your soft skills (compassion, drive, patience); combine them with the hard skills listed above. To determine your limitations, use the same techniques as above to find areas that are underdeveloped and need strengthening. Once you have completed the above task, sell your strengths and minimize your limitations. Example: Strength: communication skills. Limitation: rapid speech (byproduct of a Yankee upbringing). Plan—be aware and conscious of speech rate while delivering my messages. No one will know, employer or otherwise, the areas of your life that need work unless you decide to tell them. Power Statement: The Road To Success Is Always Under Construction.

4. Declare What You Don't Want to Do: Fact: I don't like okra. Therefore, I don't eat okra, I enjoy collards instead. If you don't like something, stop pursuing it. First step, declare three areas that you have zero interest in working. Let your flood gates open and list the industries, environments and job titles that you have zero interest. Next step, do not apply for an opportunity in any of the areas you have listed in this exploration. If you don't want to work nights and weekends, then don't pursue the service industry (management or otherwise). If you have a more circular personality and need freedom and energy from others, don't look for opportunities in a linear environment where order and routine is the norm. Your declarations will release you to pursue those areas where your interest, gifts, talents, and strengths can shine. Retention is more important than recruitment. Power Statement: When You Love What You Do, You Will Never be Forced to Go to Work Everyday.

5. *Acknowledge Your Power Source*: In our academic pursuits, relationships, and work lives, most of our actions are determined by some form of motivation. In other words, "If I do this…what's in it for me?" To find the origins of your motivation, consider these questions: Are you internally or externally focused? What motivates your successes? What compels you to select particular programs? What drives you? What fuels your passion? What keeps you connected to the things you love to do? Knowing where your passion originates is a career selling point. Some industries are looking for internal motivation, (helping profession, education, sciences, and arts). Other industries need the externally motivated, (PR/marketing, entertainment, business, legal profession). A quick note of caution: understand that your "fuel source" must be replenished or you will run on empty. The technical term for not refueling is "burnout"—don't let it happen to you. Power Statement: Find Your Life's Work, Not a Work Life!

6. *Deliver Your Ambition and Accomplishments:* Today's employers are looking for that top 10 – 30 percent employee who can perform in the marketplace. Make sure you have what it takes to meet their needs. Be a "performer," not just a "presenter." Be an "employee," not just a "candidate." Expect HR associates to dig deeper and ask questions regarding performance, achievements, initiative and leadership potential. Hiring managers and recruiters are aware that candidates can shine in a one-hour interview, but what about the long haul? You must showcase your accomplishments, how you achieved them, and your next steps. Be prepared to demonstrate your contributions, and to talk about the projects you have managed and how you "stepped out of the boat" at various levels (individual, group,

community). To have nothing won't do. If you are struggling in the performance/accomplishment area, now is the time to get on top of that. Get involved and become active in the community. Join professional groups and associations. Find volunteer opportunities that meet your life mission and academic standards. Don't just take a back seat; secure a position of leadership and develop those skills and accomplishments. Power Statement: Work Like You Have a Purpose.

7. Manage "Your" Business: Successful people see themselves as an enterprise; they act and think like a business. They value performance, change management, accomplishments, quality, self-management, time-management, community service, and reputation. You are a business—an enterprise with a quality based product line, and skilled knowledge base. Your resume should function as your brochure, highlighting your strengths and minimizing your limitations. Your interviews are to be considered "sales" meeting where you share your core products (passion, purpose, personality, potential, and performance) with a potential vendor. Your image, dress, and conduct should be consistent with your business standards. Your follow-up contact (thank you letter and/or follow-up call) will close the deal, and leave a lasting professional impression on the employer. Membership does have its privileges. Join the "Top 10–30 percent Club" or settle for the average career seeker club—you decide. Power Statement: Your Reputation Will Outweigh a Resume Any Day!

Francina R. Harrison, MSW, "The Career Engineer," is a graduate of Norfolk State University School of Social Work and the owner of Harrison & Associates, a career/business consulting business in Virginia Beach, Va. She is the author of, A Mind to Work: The Life and Career Planning Guide for People Who ~~Want~~ Need to Work (ISBN: 0-595-30390-0) and creator of the Don't Get Anxious, Get Prepared audio CD set. You may visit her website at www.thecareerengineers.com.

Kalin Thomas on Travel, the Ultimate Education

My very first time on an airplane was as a college student at Howard University in 1982. I was flying with a fellow student and my journalism professor to Milwaukee for the annual Society of Professional Journalists conference. I had been traveling with my family by car for years, but I was the first in my immediate family to take a flight, and in a way I felt like a pioneer. As the plane took off, I sang in my head the U.S. Army song *Up We Go, Into the Wild Blue Yonder*, a song I continue to sing in my head with every flight. If that had been the only long-distance trip I had taken, I would have still been a better person for it. I learned a lot of things about myself: I loved flying, I loved seeing new places and meeting new people, I loved trying regional foods, and I could hold my own at a convention where African-Americans could be counted on two hands. In essence, that trip was part of my education.

After graduating, I was hired by CNN, and moved to Atlanta. Again, I was the first in my immediate family to leave my hometown of Baltimore to live in a new city. This time I traveled by train. Though I was sad to leave my family, my sadness was outweighed by my pioneer spirit and the excitement of traveling to a new destination. As the train clicketty-clacked its way to Atlanta, I had 14 hours to dream about what my new city would be like. Is racism in the South as bad as they say? I wondered. Would the people be friendly? Would they have steamed crabs like we do in Baltimore? Would I be back home in a year?

Well, 23 years later, I'm still here, but Atlanta has become a homebase to my travels. I eventually became a producer and correspondent for CNN's weekly travel program. That dream job took me to various countries on six continents—including Antarctica. And it is through traveling that I have received my real education.

In Tokyo, Japan businessmen talked to my male colleagues instead of to me. I learned that in their culture businesswomen defer to the men in the room. I also learned that the first thing you do when greeting Japanese businessmen is present your business card—with both hands. In Santiago, Chile I was a curiosity to many locals. But even with my tiny bits of Spanish, I was able to communicate with them and found them to be warm and friendly. On a cruise to Antarctica, I found that not many black people venture to this continent. I was the only African-American on the cruise—including among the workers—but it was a trip of a lifetime. And like many trips, it reminded me that we African-Americans need to make up for lost time when it comes to world travel. In Argentina, I learned the Tango and also learned that my African hips help me catch the rhythm to just about any dance. Stepping foot on the African continent was a dream come true. And in South Africa I learned that Soweto was more than just a township of shanty houses, but also had a large black middle class with very nice homes—something you don't see in the U.S. media. One of my favorite places to visit is the Caribbean. The people are warm and friendly, and black women are celebrated for their voluptuous, African curves. And finally, I learned that as an African-American I represent my race and my country wherever I go, and I accept that reality with pleasure.

After 17 years at CNN, I was downsized during a company merger, but that didn't stop my travels. I started my own multimedia production company, and continue to travel and write about my experiences. Who would have thought my first take-off, at Washington National Airport more than 20 years ago, would lead to hundreds of take-offs to wonderful places around this country and the world. My travels have taught me the following:

- Traveling opens your mind to appreciating and respecting diverse cultures.
- African and African-American culture has touched almost every corner of this world.
- I carry the strength and the dreams of my ancestors whenever I travel, and I have the right to visit and feel safe on every continent in this world.
- My treatment around the world varies by the response to my race, my gender, and my nationality, but for the most part the world is a very welcoming place.
- It's hard to see a natural wonder like the Grand Canyon and not feel the presence of a higher power.
- Educating people about diverse cultures is part of my life's purpose.
- Travel is a means to bringing peace around the world, and I believe women will be a large part of making that happen.

Once you graduate from college, your education is just beginning; one of the best ways to get it is through travel. And don't let money be an excuse. You can learn a lot just by driving to a new place outside of your hometown. There is no better way to learn about the world, your race, your gender, your spirit, and your purpose in life than through traveling. So see the world—it's waiting for you!

Kalin Thomas is a producer, writer, photographer, consultant, and speaker. To learn more about Kalin and her multimedia company, visit www.seetheworldproductions.com.

Kimberly Taylor on Defeating Discrimination at Work

My journey through the educational system began in the Department of Defense Dependent School System. As a teen, I attended General H.H. Arnold High School in Wiesbaden, Germany. After graduating from high school, I matriculated at Texas State University-San Marcos.

I worked at my first post-college job for five years. At the company, which was in the gas detection industry, I was in the center of a white, male-dominated industry. Therefore, as a woman I was an anomaly. And as a young, African-American woman, often times I was not initially taken seriously. I loved the job, but the price of a white collar lifestyle was taxing. I was treated with lady-like respect and I was expected to work as hard as a man, but when I asked for the same opportunities as a man I was denied.

I experienced a situation where I had taken several business trips to the West Coast and reported to my sales manager the status of our product and the needs of our distributors in California. I explained to him that the regional sales manager was still not living up to his commitment to our company and that I had been asked by several high dollar customers (including managers at Exxon) to visit them personally. I also explained that the trip to meet with the gas executives would be an excellent pretext to my going into outside sales. My manager dismissed my report and stated that I wasn't ready for outside sales. I was truly upset and depressed to the point of wanting to quit. Ultimately, I felt debased because a younger man in the inside sales department—who I had two years experience over—was being sent into outside sales. He was by no means better at the job. Our management was covertly expressing an inferiority complex about women.

After my experience, I prayed about what I should do. I stayed. I knew that one day my glory would come. As I continued my work with this company, I eventually asked for a review to discuss an additional raise after two years of exemplary service. My manager kept dodging me and I felt he was not trying hard enough to help with my situation, so I discussed the matter with the vice-president (it was a very small office). The next day my manager had a conference with me. He stated that our clients felt I was being rude and I kept people on hold on the telephone for lengthy amounts of time. He said that he was speaking to me because the problem was critical. I immediately told him that he was lying. I had received a review not three weeks prior to our meeting, which was rated perfect. If there was a problem, I would've known.

Every issue he brought up, I shot down. He said he would review me in 30 days and every 30 days afterwards. I felt despondent and hurt. I knew he was retaliating against me because I had asked for a raise and spoken with the vice-president. In my worldly days I would have cursed his name, quit, sought revenge or had an evil spirit about me. Instead, I documented all his accusations, and I interviewed the people who "complained" about my so-called poor performance. Everyone denied the negative statements. I knew I was an outstanding worker. I boldly turned the findings into my manager's boss and the company's president. I stayed on the job and I was nice to my manager.

Ultimately, I never received a follow-up review and my manager was demoted to a regular inside sales position for poor work. Two months later, he was fired. I, on the other hand, was promoted to supervisor and given a substantial raise. My persecution on the job is just one of the many examples of discrimination in the workplace. It will occur whether it is because of age, color, or gender. As long as African-Americans continue to move into the middle and upper class, we will always be targets. Stand strong and never give up your integrity. Never let anyone walk over you.

Kimberly Taylor is a graduate of Texas State University-San Marcos.

Marshawn Evans on Choosing to be Bitter or Better

With the job market being so touch-and-go, more people are finding themselves the victims of cutbacks and firings. To a certain extent, I too have suffered several disappointments in my professional life.

In 2001, I had the honor of becoming Miss District of Columbia, representing the nation's capital at the Miss America competition. Even though I finished as the third runner-up, winning the talent (as a baton twirler) and interviewing awards, and acquiring more than $50,000 in scholarships for law school, what I really wanted was to win the title of Miss America.

When I returned from the pageant, I was in the middle of a fellowship funded by the U.S. Justice Department. It ended a few months early, leaving me essentially without regular work—my second disappointment. I was not fired but it sure felt like it. I took this "time off" as an opportunity to start Communication Counts!, a public speaking consulting company. At the age of 22, I was able to travel across the country conducting seminars, delivering keynote speeches for conferences and corporations, and training clients to enhance their communication and interviewing skills. Had I won the job of Miss America and if my fellowship had not ended early, I would not have had the time, desire or ability to focus on starting a business.

Recently, I received what some might view as another letdown when I was publicly fired as one of the candidates on "The

Apprentice." However, being fired by Donald Trump on national TV has its advantages. I've been able to launch a national speaking tour, conduct seminars, work on books, start an inspirational clothing line, purchase my first home and begin practicing as an attorney.

Behind every obstacle is an opportunity. It's not the challenges we face that determine our future, but how we face them. Having multiple dynamics to your life helps you move past challenges quicker and with more focus. You can choose to be bitter or better. Successful people always choose the latter. I've learned that problems present an opportunity for your purpose and passion to let loose. So to prepare for those disappointing times in life:

Find Your Passion: Discover what you do extraordinarily well and cultivate it. Have several back-up plans that reflect your talents, experience and connections. When the right opportunity comes along you will be ready to execute your skill set.

Follow Your Heart: Intuition is powerful. Don't underestimate yourself, overthink, or be afraid to chart your own course!

Focus: See the bigger picture in the midst of adversity—whether it's being fired or frustrated with your job. You can always turn a problem into a possibility if you're focused on the future. Setbacks are often set-ups for success in disguise.

* reprinted with permission from Upscale magazine.

Marshawn Evans, a graduate of Georgetown University, is an attorney, professional speaker, author and on-air personality. For more information about her visit www.marshawnevans.com.

Lola Brown on Grad School Journeys: 12 Rounds to Victory

My favorite athlete is Laila Ali. What makes her unique is that she is a smart athlete. She knows how to win in any environment she's in. She knows she needs to pull her hair back in order to win a fight in the ring, but she also knows when to put on an incredible dress to win adoration at a red carpet event. And regardless of the atmosphere, she plans out her moves.

While Laila's opponent may have been Jackie Frazier, I faced a handful of contenders in my own personal ring. Difficult coursework, school politics, negative competition and people's ulterior motives all stood in my way of obtaining a graduate degree. But Laila and I both had training, coaching, mentoring, perseverance in times of challenge, discipline, and an outright will to beat our opponent. The other thing we both had was motivation, a reason to win. Most likely, one of her reasons for trying to beat Jackie Frazier was to uphold the Ali boxing legacy. My motivation, however, was a little different.

Warm-up Round

Since high school, my passion has been to find the cure for sickle cell anemia. It was something that struck me from the moment I was sitting in my biology class my junior year, learning how the disease so severely impacted the quality of life of the people who were affected by this disease, many of who are people of color. Even today, it still touches my heart to reflect on the strength and will people with sickle cell anemia have. I felt it would be an honor to use my God given intellect to help find a cure for this disease. So after graduating from Brown University with a degree in biology, I entered graduate school at Georgia Tech with a passion, will, and desire to help find a cure for sickle cell anemia.

Against the Ropes

While the beginning of my graduate school experience started off well, over time, my relationship with my advisor as well as the challenges in finding a suitable project began to become a problem. We had a difficult time communicating, and I soon learned that without an appropriate advisor (coach), the likelihood of success would become increasingly difficult. I soon became very frustrated and depressed about my situation and did not know what to do. I was at a point where I needed help desperately, but at the same time I felt like I was letting down the people that were cheering me on, as well as the people with sickle cell anemia that I could potentially help. I didn't want to share my feelings with my classmates because I thought they might think I couldn't keep up. As an African-American woman I felt an added pressure to succeed because the number of women of color studying or working in the sciences is so low, and I did not want to be an example of someone that could not make the cut. I later learned, however, that some of my peers were having the same difficulties I was experiencing.

Still, at the time, I was lost and did not know what to do. So I did the only thing I knew to do—I prayed. I prayed for someone that would help me regain focus and assist me in seeing the incredible scientist that was inside of me. I became very attentive to people around me, asking if they knew of people that could give me advice for my situation.

12th Round Turnaround

Not long after I decided to pray for assistance, a visiting faculty came to the biomedical engineering department. She was an African-American woman, and one of the few black faculty members at the university. Ironically, she was an expert in sickle cell anemia and had developed a device created to study sickle cell anemia that is routinely used among medical researchers today. I knew this was my opportunity to change my situation, and I was prepared to take advantage of it. I immediately introduced myself to her upon her first days in the lab, and what I thought would be a brief five minute introduction turned into a two-hour long conversation about my research, the grad school experience for African-American women in the science and engineering, and our personal and professional goals.

Dr. Barabino and I had an incredible connection, both professionally and personally, and I quickly recognized and ingested her wisdom like a sponge. She saw me as a student with talent and ability, and was willing to help me develop focus on my project. In turn, I was a person that she felt comfortable around and could share her experiences in academia as a trailblazer in her field. She soon became my co-advisor and career mentor. She taught me a tremendous amount about the intangible skills of graduate school—how to talk about my research in formal and informal settings, and how to show confidence in my project as the first African-American female student in the department. Above all these things, however, the biggest thing Dr. Barabino did for me was show belief in my ability. She continually encouraged and supported me through a time when I had doubts about my potential. Her belief in my ability gave me the confidence to know I could be, and already was to a degree, an excellent scientist. Having graduate school challenges early on, I was at a point where my confidence was waning, but getting encouragement and support from someone who had accomplished so much in her professional career was that intangible 'x' factor that turned my graduate school experience around.

Technical Knockout

With Dr. Barabino's support and guidance, I gained my second wind. I was reenergized, and ready to go back in the trenches and get the degree. In less than one year, I developed an original project, completed all the experiments, analyzed all the data, wrote an extensive thesis, and defended it successfully before my thesis committee and peers. By doing this, I became the first African-American woman to receive a master's degree from Georgia Tech, one of the top three biomedical engineering programs in the country. Additionally, my thesis work achieved a childhood dream: to help demystify the complexity of sickle cell anemia, and contribute to finding a cure to this disease.

Post Fight Commentary

As I reflect upon my graduate school experience, I realized there were several key steps I took to make my graduate school experience more successful. You can also use these steps to succeed in whatever graduate program you are in.

1. Network proactively: When I saw that Dr. Barabino was on campus, I immediately went to talk to her. At the time, I didn't know how long she would there, but I was ready to make the most of the time that she was there to solicit her assistance. What was also critical was that I was already prepared to talk to her; I could clearly articulate where I needed help and how I thought she might be able to help me. It's vital to be clear and to the point with people you want assistance from. Most of them are very busy, and seeming uncertain or being vague sometimes shows a lack of forethought.

2. Capitalize on strong relationships: What made my interaction with Dr. Barabino so incredible was that we had a personal and professional connection. Because there are such a small number of African-American women in science and engineering pursuing advanced degrees, we had an instant connection. She helped me tremendously by giving me an incredible amount of her time and advice as a seasoned, highly recognized scientist, but I was actually able to help her too in that I was able to listen to and relate to her experiences as an African-American female scientist. This provided an incredible foundation, and it then seemed quite natural for her to become my career mentor and official co-advisor. My relationship with Dr. Barabino did not stop when I got my master's degree. Dr. Barabino went on to assist me in looking for a job, she critiqued my resume, gave me leads and contacts, and assisted me with preparing for my job interviews.

3. Get a smart game plan: I believe in working smart, then working hard. You have to know when you have to buckle down and work hard, and when you can rest a little bit. It's about being strategic. Once I had clearly defined my thesis project, I had to make a plan on how I would map out my time in order to get all my experiments done, analyze the data, and write my thesis. Before making any major steps, I always touched base with Dr. Barabino to ask one basic question: Am I doing this in the most efficient way possible? The last thing I wanted to do was work hard on something just to realize I could have done it quicker or better if I had done it another way. I never skimped out on working hard; I just planned out where and when I had to focus my energy in order to get everything done.

4. Realize what you are not in control over: Most of us work so hard, trying to make decisions that will give us the best opportunity for success. But in some cases we will find that our efforts simply aren't enough and there is something that we don't yet possess to achieve the success we're yearning for; in other words, the problem is out of our hands. Once we do everything we can, we must be comfortable in letting it go and moving forward. Once I had prayed for help with my situation, I knew I had done everything I could do and I began to have confidence that my problem was already solved, and prepared myself for the person that would help me turn my situation around.

There are additional important actions to take when planning a successful graduate school experience:

1. Get a good coach: People give different pieces of advice on how to choose an advisor, but I recommend looking at the following things when identifying your grad school advisor:

- Make sure your personality is similar to that of your potential advisor. You should be able to look at your advisor and think, "This is the kind of professional I would like to be when I have completed my degree." Think about your advisor's leadership style, and his or her interaction with colleagues and other students.

- Talk to the advisor's past and current students. Current students will usually be honest with you about their experience with their advisor, but sometimes they may say negative things in a covert way. Other times, they just will not be honest. That's why I say talk to past students as well. If your advisor does not have the contact information for his/her former students, you should wonder why. The inference is that they do not keep in contact with their former students, which is atypical. Former students will almost always give you their honest opinion because they have less to lose if they say something negative. Former students will also give you an overall perspective of how their graduate school experience impacted their career.

2. Network: Networking is very important during your grad school experience. Introduce yourself to as many people as possible, regardless of whether they are doing something you are interested in. Build a strong rapport with students and faculty alike because you do not know when you will be able to be a resource for them, or better yet, when they can be a resource for you.

I am now a research scientist at Emory University in Atlanta, Georgia. I realize that I have been afforded many benefits that came as a direct result of having gone to graduate school. I was able to secure a higher position and salary than my colleagues who only had bachelor's degrees. As a result of my training in grad school, I immediately looked for and saw things I could do to improve the scientific and organizational structure of the lab, and this led to increased productivity and independence. I am much more apt to express my opinion as it relates to science, and am confident in the scientific explanations I give because of the presentations I gave before faculty in grad school. Additionally, I am aware of my talents and what I am worth as an employee, and am not afraid to ask for what I need or deserve in a professional manner.

If given the opportunity to turn the hands of time and make the decision whether to go to grad school, I would go every time. I look at my time in grad school as preparation for becoming a stronger scientist and developing persistence in achieving my goals. And as with boxing, the journey to my victory has taught me far more than I ever would have realized—about what it means to have heart, to never give up, and having the will to win.

Lola Brown is a research scientist, mentor and educator. You may visit her website, www.lolabrown.org.

Mavis Gragg on
Finding Yourself in Unexpected Places

When I was a little girl I would stand in front of the large mirror in the hall bathroom and stare at myself. I would stare so long that it would soon begin to seem as if I was looking at a different person. Who is that girl? Does she talk like me, walk like me, act like me? Why does she look like that? Who will she be when she is 12, 16, 21, or old? Is this really me? These are all questions that would come to mind as I looked back at the tall, warm brown figure in the mirror.

As I look at that same girl in the mirror, now 30 years old, I know exactly who she is and I love her! It took a long time for me to get to this point, however, and it took taking some risks.

The summer of 2002 was a typical stifling-hot North Carolina summer, only I spent it in the cool comfort of air conditioning with my head buried in bar study books. I had just finished law school and was preparing to finally become an adult. My plan was to pass the Georgia bar (hopefully) and move to the urban utopia for black professionals—Atlanta. My understanding was that Atlanta was a place where people could make their dreams come true. You could make lots of money, buy a McMansion, and find love. Yet, during those seemingly endless hours of focusing on law and my future, something did not feel quite right. The same questions I had as a child began to haunt me. One was particularly troubling: Is this really me?

I did not have to look far to get the initial answer. When I wasn't memorizing torts and constitutional law or honing my multiple choice question answering skills, I was able to spend some time escaping with Langston Hughes' *I Wonder as I Wander,* his autobiography about his travels around the globe in the 1920s, and Elaine Lee's *Go Girl: The Black Woman's Book of Travel and Adventure.* These two books were my connection to the world I was missing while holed up in the library. The authors' adventurous stories warmed my soul because they were of people who took non-traditional paths to happiness, and some of those paths took them to the corners of the globe. Their stories inspired a shift in how I thought about my immediate future. I decided that I would hop off the straight and narrow path I had been taking my whole life to discover who I really was. I thought the best way to do this would be through traveling. I hoped my new path would take me out of my comfort zone, and perhaps even my time zone.

My first challenge was to get my parents' help. I knew in order to travel I would have to have their approval and I would have to move home to save up the funds for my experience. My parents were very proud of my accomplishments and excited for the future that awaited me in Atlanta. So, when I contacted them three weeks before the bar exam I think they found my news and request quite perplexing. Still, their love and support was unconditional and they welcomed me home with open arms after I wrapped up my bar exam.

Preparing for my big adventure was not as easy as I thought. I secured a nice job at a community mediation center, but it didn't pay very much. I decided to take on contract work with an online mediation firm to supplement my savings. My other dilemma was that I did not know where on Earth I wanted to go to find myself. The world is so vast and deciding where to travel was a daunting task. However, my previous travel experiences helped me narrow down a few requirements for my destination. I liked a good exchange rate on the dollar. I liked good food and exciting social scenes. I did not like hostels nor did I like being around too many gringos (tourists). I liked Europe, but I had been there once in 1996 for a month and then for a semester in 2000. Most important, I knew I wanted to be around black people. Thus, I knew it was time to go below the equator.

As if by fate, another Friday night at home had me surfing the television and I struck gold. Rather, I struck Samba! The Sundance Channel was featuring a documentary called *E Minha Cara/That's My Face*, which was eloquently done by Thomas Allen Harris. In this film, Harris allows the viewers to tag along in his spiritual journey to Salvador de Bahia, Brazil, a city known as the heart and soul of black Brazil. It seemed like heaven to me. So, it was set. I would go to Salvador de Bahia.

First, I met with my lone Brazilian friend, Erica, who gave me the rundown on Salvador de Bahia, which she loved. I decided I would go to the city for three months and have the flexibility of staying longer if I wanted. Erica helped me create a budget. I was pleasantly surprised when she told me I would only need $3,500. That was including the flight, accommodations at a nice poussada (guest house), food, and fun.

Erica then referred me to a travel agency that specializes in airfare to Brazil, and she hooked me up with her friend Lily who taught Brazilian Portuguese. Lily and I began one-on-one lessons in March of 2004, a little over three months before my departure. To further prepare myself I read travel books to figure out what to pack, how to move about, and what to see and do.

June 13th arrived in no time, but six months of planning and learning Portuguese could not prepare me for what I would experience in Salvador. The first three weeks were not easy at all. The shock of unfamiliarity hit me hard as I found myself in a place with different smells, sounds, and all new faces. I found security in latching on to what was familiar: the mall, chocolate, my music, and my room at the Poussada Azul. Once I became friendly with the staff at the Poussada, I tried to get some help connecting with the outside world. Their response, however, was disappointing. "Vocé é Brasiliera!" they told me. You are

Brazilian.

I retreated back to my room and began journaling, reading, doubting and then crying. I thought I was lost—not just in this foreign place but in life. Who puts off a potentially profitable career as an attorney to travel thousands of miles away from what they know? Me. She comes all the way to this "Black Rome" and has a three-week pity party, I thought to myself.

But an invitation to lunch changed my fate. Three degrees of separation from my best friend in Charlotte, North Carolina connected me to another lady living in Salvador. She too was a lawyer. She too decided to take a different path. And she introduced me to other black women who were doing what felt right for them. One was working on her Ph.D. in history. One was working on her Ph.D. in cultural anthropology. One had a consulting business. And though it seemed odd, all of them—all of us—were in the best place on earth to do all of these things.

With the help of my newfound friends I finally truly stepped out of my comfort zone and opened up my heart and mind to embrace the lifestyle of a native. I found that Salvador lived up to its reputation. Home to more than three million people, mostly black, there is always something going on in Salvador. Every day I heard live music and danced. I looked forward to each opportunity to catch the spirit at soccer game viewings (a major pastime in Brazil) and to lounge at the beach. In between those fun excursions I enjoyed the conversations with my friends. Sometimes we were highly intellectual; other times we were silly and playful. We always enlightened each other and encouraged each other's dreams.

I returned to the States very aware of myself, and with more self-determination than any degree or job could give me. By the end of my summer in Salvador I had learned a few things about me. I learned I am *somebody* (a la Jesse Jackson). I learned that I can adapt to change. I also learned I am cute (especially in skirts), and I can dance in the streets rain or shine. But the most important thing I learned was that sometimes you have to do what may seem counter-intuitive in order to learn more about yourself and to grow. By this I mean that the girl in the mirror may have had questions or doubts about who she was, but all it took was taking some risks—stepping out into the world—and she was able to get affirmation and learn new things.

I am now an attorney and mediator. I believe I am a better professional because I allowed myself to really discover who I was and become more confident that I was on the right path. I make sure to keep things flavorful and continue to create opportunities to learn by traveling and dabbling in different hobbies and activities. Since the summer of 2004 I have returned to Brazil twice, including for Carnaval 2006. I have also traveled to Ghana and Coite D'Ivoire. I dance, collect new music, experiment with mixed media art, and more.

Finding Yourself Through Travel

I found myself through traveling and you can too. I find it helpful when planning a trip or any project to have a mock conversation about the experience in past tense. Be creative here. When I began preparing for Brazil my conversation went something like this: "My experience in Brazil was so amazing! I learned about the history and culture of the Afro-Brazilians. I am conversational in Portuguese. I now know how to dance the Samba and I can do Capoeira. I have collected a lot of new music. I made some great friends who will forever hold a special place in my heart. The food was amazing and I even learned how to cook some new dishes. I stayed healthy the whole time—no cooties! My accommodations were comfortable and affordable. I felt comfortable with my finances and did not return broke. In fact, I bought some great new jewelry and clothes! And just as important, I learned something new every day."

From this conversation you can then create categories that will help you structure your goals and tasks to make the trip happen. Within mine I knew there was "Social Activities," "Finances," "Connections," "Instruction/Classes," "Touristy Things." Under each category I then put tasks, e.g. learn

Portuguese, save XX dollars, investigate possible connections in Brazil, learn about sizing in clothes, and make a list of must-see museums, organizations, and places. Once I had the tasks written down I could determine how I would accomplish each task and track my progress. For example, I knew that to avoid returning from my experience broke, I would have to save up cushion money in addition to money for my trip or find a way to work remotely, which I did by continuing to mediate online. I chose to learn Portuguese from a private teacher who gave me her undivided attention. I knew it was unrealistic for me to try and learn with CDs or a class. I got lots of vaccinations and over-the-counter drugs. I also put out an alert to my close connections that I wanted to be connected to anyone who had anything to do with Brazil and could help me. Planning this way was tremendously important in order for me to have the experience I desired. Still, you cannot expect that your plans will fall exactly into place. When I first arrived in Salvador I felt uncomfortable, and I did not accomplish all of my goals, per se. However, by having a vision of what I wanted to happen and good information, I was able to move towards a beautiful experience.

Mavis Gragg was born and raised in Black Mountain, North Carolina. She earned a bachelor of arts degree in industrial relations from the University of North Carolina at Chapel Hill, and also holds a juris doctor and master's degree in dispute resolution from Pepperdine University School of Law. She is currently an analyst for a litigation consulting firm in her beloved North Carolina.

The ABC's of Embracing the Real World

"Life is a marvelous, transitory adventure."
—Nikki Giovanni

Everyone has to live and learn in their career and in life, but no one said you couldn't be helped along the way! I hope *Embracing the Real World: The Black Woman's Guide to Life After College* has been an informational and inspirational tool for you. The "ABC's Of Embracing the Real World" was created to reiterate advice given throughout the book.

A: Ask For What You Want: A person who is afraid to ask for what they want will miss out on a lot of opportunities. Make your goals and aspirations known to the people who can help you in your endeavors, no matter how big or small.

B: Be Better Than Your Competition: Know who your competition is and make sure you're five steps ahead of what they know and what they've done, so all eyes will be on you when it's time to get promoted or singled out for a better job with a better company.

C: Challenge Yourself To Do More Than What's Expected of You: It's the people who go above and beyond what's asked of them who are recognized as leaders in their industries and the pillars of their communities. Do more than what's merely expected of you and the rewards you reap will be more than what you expected.

D: Develop Good Relationships With Your Co-Workers: You don't have to be buddy-buddy with everyone in the office, but you do need to maintain a good working relationship with everyone from the secretary to the CEO. You never know who you might depend on for something you need in the future.

E: Expect To Have Some Very Bad Days: Sometimes you might be two seconds away from quitting your job, or seriously hurting someone. Realize that bad days on the job are inevitable and learn how to stay composed and in control when nothing seems to be going right.

F: Forget What The Naysayers Said: You've made it this far despite all the negative and unsupportive words and gestures of others. Continue to strive for what's in your best interest, and surround yourself with people who want to see you succeed and will help you any way they can.

G: Get Your Wardrobe Together: "Dress to impress" is not just a catchy phrase. Your appearance is the first thing a person notices and you should dress appropriately for your job.

H: Highlight Your Achievements: Don't be bashful about tooting your own horn. No one will know of your achievements unless you tell them.

I: Identify Areas You Need To Improve Upon: There will always be skills you need to sharpen and ones you need to develop to make yourself more marketable. Never become complacent and think you've learned all you need to learn and know everything you need to know.

J: Join Professional Organizations: The networking opportunities you'll find through professional organizations are extremely valuable. There's truth in the famous phrase, "It's not what you know, but who you know."

K: Keep Your Private Business Private: It's okay to have a close friend at the office who you can share personal details of your life with during lunch, but everyone shouldn't know what you do once you leave the office—about your financial woes, or about your crazy ex-boyfriend. And though your co-workers may be very interested in hearing about all your latest trials and tribulations, they are bound to wonder why you have such a big mouth and why you don't keep your private business private.

L: Learn The Art Of Negotiation: Whether you realize it or not, you've been negotiating for what you want all of your life. You had to convince someone to give you a later curfew, change your C to a B, let you have the bigger bedroom, and so on. Whether you got what you wanted in the past depended on how well you stated your case. And what you want now and in the future—a raise, better benefits, more responsibility—will also depend on how persuasive you are. Practice negotiating for things you know won't just get handed to you, and buy a book on how to negotiate.

M: Maintain A Positive Image & Attitude: You never know who is watching you from a distance after five, and what stranger you had an attitude with will be the one smirking as they interview you for a job. Always treat everyone with courtesy and respect, and present yourself as an intelligent, poised and professional individual who others would be lucky to know.

N: Never Compromise Your Values: There will be some decisions others will make that rub you the wrong way, and perhaps you will be asked to do something that you wouldn't if given the choice—that's life and accept it. However, if a decision someone else has made keeps you tossing and turning at night, or if you're asked to do something that goes against your core values, morals or religious beliefs, that's life too but you don't have to accept it. You shouldn't do anything that you feel compromises your integrity or something that you wholeheartedly believe is wrong. And you don't need to work for anyone that would ask or tell you to do things that are not in your best interest or are morally unsound.

O: Overcome Your Insecurities: You are beautiful, you are smart, you are capable, and you do have something to offer the world. But do you know it? Your insecurities will keep you from succeeding in life. The sooner you get to working on being secure with yourself, the sooner your success will come.

P: Prioritize Your Goals: List your goals in order of importance and have a reasonable time line that shows when you should have each goal accomplished. Do this so that you won't be trying to get too many things done at once, and then get nothing done at all.

Q: Question What You Don't Understand: Don't go around assuming anything, and don't be afraid to ask people things you think you should know already. Learn to speak up and speak your mind, and you'll be a more knowledgeable person for it.

R: Realize Your Worth & Potential: You have it going on and that's the unconceited truth. To be young, black and gifted is a wonderful thing—to be a black educated woman with a good head on her shoulders is a dream come true. Realize that whole worlds of possibilities are yours to explore, and the only thing that can truly limit you is your underestimation of yourself.

S: Say What You Mean & Mean What You Say: Be straightforward and honest about your feelings. You'll gain the respect of others and prevent people from misunderstanding you or not taking what you say seriously.

T: Trust Your Intuition: Learn to listen to and trust that little voice inside your head that tells you when something isn't quite right or what the best choice will be concerning a decision you have to make.

U: Use Your Talents: Don't let your talents go to waste. Find a way to use them, whatever they may be, to enrich your life and the lives of others.

V: Vocalize Your Concerns: If something is seriously bothering you at work don't be afraid to tactfully talk to the person who can address your concerns; chances are that others may be frustrated with something going on in your company too.

W: Waste No Time In Following Your Dreams: Start actively pursuing your goals and dreams today, even if you can only take small steps in going after what you want right now.

X: X-amine Your Work: Look critically at your work before others do. Make sure you are measuring up to the standards set by your company and that your work truly exemplifies your talent.

Y: Yearn For Something More: Don't settle for anything; mediocrity is not your friend. Expect the best for yourself and always be on the lookout for ways you can improve yourself and your life.

Z: Zone In On What Matters Most To You: It's what you want for your career and life that should matter most to you—not the desires of your parents, love interest or employers. You won't get any satisfaction from your achievements if you pursued them to make someone else happy.

Resource Guide

BOOKS

Bramson, Robert. *What Your Boss Doesn't Tell You Until It's Too Late: How to Correct Behavior That Is Holding You Back.* Fireside, 1996.

Brooks, Donna and Brooks, Lynn. *Seven Secrets of Successful Women: Success Strategies of the Women Who Have Made It—And How You Can Follow Their Lead.* McGraw-Hill, 1999.

Broussard, Cheryl. *The Black Woman's Guide to Financial Independence: Smart Ways to Take Charge of Your Money, Build Wealth, and Achieve Financial Security.* Penguin 1996.

Evans, Gail. *Play Like a Man Win Like a Woman: What Men Know About Success that Women Need to Learn.* Broadway, 2000.

Foley, Mary. *Bodacious. An AOL Insider Cracks the Code to Outrageous Success for Women.* Amacon, 2002.

Frankel, Lois. *Nice Girls Don't Get Rich: 75 Avoidable Mistakes Women Make with Money.* Warner Business Books, 2005.

Frankel, Lois. *Nice Girls Don't Get the Corner Office: 101 Unconscious Mistakes Women Make That Sabotage Their Careers.* Warner Business Books, 2004.

Ginsburg Wood, Karen. *Don't Sabotage Your Success! Make Office Politics Work.* Enlightened Concepts Pub, 2000.

Gray, John. *How to Get What You Want at Work: A Practical Guide for Improving Communication and Getting Results.* Harper Paperbacks, 2003.

Greenwood, Monique. *Having What Matters: The Black Woman's Guide to Creating the Life You Really Want.* William Morrow, 2001.

Hansen, Katharine. *Dynamic Cover Letters for New Graduates.* Ten Speed Press, 1998.

Harrison, Francina. *A Mind to Work: The Life and Career Planning Guide for People Who ~~Want~~ Need to Work!* iUniverse, 2004.

Hill, Napoleon. *Think and Grow Rich.* Aventine Press, 2004.

Kolb, Deborah, et. al. *Her Place at the Table: A Woman's Guide to Negotiating Five Key Challenges to Leadership Success.* Jossey-Bass, 2004.

Levit, Alexandra. *They Don't Teach Corporate in College: A Twenty-Something's Guide to the Business World.* Career Press, 2004.

Lichtenberg, Ronna. *Pitch Like a Girl: How a Woman Can Be Herself and Still Succeed.* Rodale Books, 2005.

Mayer, Jeffrey. *Success Is A Journey: Seven Steps to Achieving Success in the Business of Life.* McGraw Hill, 2001.

McGinty, Sarah. *Power Talk: Using Language to Build Authority and Influence.* Warner Business Books, 2001.

McIntyre, Marie G. *Secrets to Winning at Office Politics: How to Achieve Your Goals and Increase Your Influence at Work.* St. Martin's Griffin, 2005.

Mindell, Phyllis. *How to Say It For Women: Communicating with Confidence and Power Using the Language of Success.* Prentice Hall Press, 2001.

Murphy, Evelyn, and E.J. Graff. *Getting Even: Why Women Don't Get Paid Like Men—And What to Do About It.* Touchstone, 2005.

Nivens, Beatryce. *Success Strategies for African-Americans: A Guide to Personal and Professional Achievement.* Plume, 1998.

Orman, Suze. *The Money Book for the Young, Fabulous & Broke.* Riverhead, 2005.

Pollan, Stephen and Levine, Mark. *Lifescripts: What to Say to Get What You Want in Life's Difficult Situations.* John Wiley & Sons, 2004.

Reals Ellig, Janice, and Bill Morin. *What Every Successful Woman Knows: 12 Breakthrough Strategies to Get the Power and Ignite Your Career.* McGraw-Hill, 2001.

Schuller, Robert. *Tough Times Never Last, But Tough People Do.* Bantam, 1984.

Scott, Susan. *Fierce Conversations: Achieving Success at Work & in Life, One Conversation at a Time.* Berkley Publishing Group, 2004.

Solomon, Muriel. *Working With Difficult People.* Prentice Hall Press, 2002.

Tracy, Brian. *Eat That Frog! 21 Great Ways to Stop Procrastinating and Get More Done in Less Time.* Hodder-Staughton, 2004.

Tracy, Brian. *Goals! How to Get Everything You Want—Faster Than You Ever Thought Possible.* Berrett-Koehler Publishers, Inc., 2003.

Wellington, Sheila, and Betty Spence. *Be Your Own Mentor: Strategies from Top Women on the Secrets of Success.* Random House, 2001.

Wingett, Larry. *Shut Up, Stop Whining, and Get a Life: A Kick-Butt Approach to a Better Life.* Wiley, 2004.

USEFUL WEBSITES

General Job Search Websites

www.ajb.dni.us
www.careerbuilder.com
www.careercity.com
www.collegegrad.com
www.craigslist.com
www.hotjobs.com
www.ihirejobnetwork.com
www.jobbankusa.com

www.jobcentral.com
www.jobs.com
www.thejobspider.com
www.monster.com
www.nettemps.com
www.quintcareers.com
www.vault.com
www.wetfeet.com
www.worktree.comne

Specialty Job Search Websites

www.accountemps.com: accounting jobs
www.bluefoxjobs.com: jobs in the casino, cruise, restarant and hotel industry
www.bookjobs.com: book publishing jobs
www.biocareer.com: biotechnology industry jobs
www.chronicle.com: higher education jobs
www.computerjobsbank.com: computer, technology and engineering jobs
www.creativegroup.com: marketing and advertising jobs
www.crewnet.com: film and television industry jobs
www.dentalpower.com: jobs in dentistry
www.developers.net: high tech jobs
www.dice.com: high tech jobs
www.fedworld.gov: federal jobs
www.govtjobs.com:government jobs
www.healthcaresource.com: healthcare jobs
www.healthcarejobs.com: healthcare jobs
www.higheredjob.com: higher education jobs
www.ihirechemists.com: chemistry jobs
www.ihirehr.com: human resources jobs
www.insidehighered.com: higher ed jobs
www.journalismnext.com: journalism jobs
www.lawcrossing.com: legal jobs
www.marketingjobs.com: sales and marketing jobs

www.mediabistro.com: media and publishing jobs
www.mediarecruiter.com: media jobs
www.mortgageboard.net: mortgage, banking, title, escrow and real estate
www.nature.com/naturejobs: science jobs in various industries
www.orasearch.com: oracle database IT jobs
www.policeemployment.com: federal, state, city and country law enforcement jobs
www.publishersmarketplace.com: publishing jobs
www.spacejobs.com: aeronautic and space industry jobs
www.telecomcareers.net: telecommunications jobs
www.usajobs.com: federal jobs
www.webjobs.com: internet jobs and links to other job sites

Websites for Women

www.bcw.org: the website of a national organization for black women in the workforce.
www.catalyst.com: the website of a research and advisory organization that conducts and publishes research on all aspects of women's career advancement.
www.ewomennetwork.com: an online network for women in business.
www.womenforhire.com: the website for an organization that offers career expos, career advice, seminars, a career-focused magazine, and an online job board.
http://www.women-21.gov: a website for women entrepreneurs.

Government Websites

www.bls.gov/oco/: a U.S. Department of Labor website that provides information on hundreds of jobs.

Websites for Career Information

www.blackcareerzone.com: provides career information for African-Americans.

www.blackcollegian.com: provides career information and a job bank for black college undergraduates.

www.careeroverview.com: provides job descriptions for hundreds of positions.

www.career-resumes.com: provides sample resumes.

www.askdrlesa.com: a website, hosted by Dr. L'esa Guilian, that offers career advice.

www.imdiversity.com: a career and self-development site for minorities.

www.salary.com: provides an abundance of information on salaries and compensation for nearly every field imaginable. The website also includes a cost-of-living and benefits calculator.

www.careerjournal.com: in-depth career website hosted by *The Wall Street Journal*.

www.collegegrad.com: in-depth career website for college grads.

www.monster.com: provide a host of career information and a job search engine.

www.statejobs.com: provides information about the country's largest employers and the best companies to work for.

www.vault.com: provides an abundance of career information, including what its like to work in different fields.

www.networkjournal.com: a magazine for Black professionals and small business owners.

Other Useful Websites

www.bankrate.com: a website that provides free rate information to consumers on more than 300 financial products, including mortgages, credit cards, new and used automobile loans, money market accounts, certificates of deposit, checking and ATM fees, home equity loans and online banking fees.

www.gradschool.com: a comprehensive online source of graduate information.

www.money.cnn.com: a CNN-run online magazine that provides personal finance information.

www.nul.org: the National Urban League's website, an organization with chapters across the country dedicated to empowering African-Americans to enter the economic and social mainstream. The organization has an auxiliary organization for young professionals.

www.ugogirl.com: the web-based home of *Go Girl: The Black Woman's Book Of Travel and Adventure*. The site also serves as a forum for the exchange of vital information among African-American travelers.

Occupational Organizations for African-Americans

www.nabsw.org: National Association of Black Social Workers
www.nabtp.org: National Association of Black Telecommunications Professionals
www.nmanet.org: National Medical Association
www.nabj.org: National Association of Black Journalists
www.nabainc.org: National Association of Black Accountants
www.ncbl.org: National Conference of Black Lawyers
www.abpsi.org: The Association of Black Psychologists
www.nabsdivers.org: National Association of Black Scuba Divers
www.nabse.org: National Alliance of Black School Educators
www.nbna.org: National Black Nurses Association
www.nbmbaa.org: National Black MBA Association
www.nsbe.org: National Association of Black Engineers

www.nabgg.com: National Association of Black
  Geologists and Geophysicists
www.naobi.org: National Association of Black
  Interpreters
www.nabsnet.org: National Association of Black
  Storytellers
www.nobcche.org: National Association for the
  Professional Advancement of Black Chemists and
  Chemical Engineers
www.noblenational.org: National Association of Black
  Law Enforcement Executives
www.aabe.org: National Association of Blacks in Energy
www.blackpolice.org: National Black Police Association
www.bcala.org: Black Caucus of the American Library
  Association, Inc.
www.aaawd.net: The Association of African-American
  Web Developers
www.naaahr.org: National Association of African-
  Americans in Human Resources
www.covchurch.org: African-American Ministers
  Association
www.bdpa.org: Black Data Processing Associates
www.nationalbar.org: National Association for Black
  Lawyers
www.obap.org: Organization of Black Airline Pilots
www.ntaonline.org: National Technical Association
www.core77.com/OBD: Organization of Black Designers
www.ndaonline.org: National Dental Association
www.abcardio.org: Association of Black Cardiologists, Inc.
www.sbas.net: The Society of Black Academic Surgeons
www.bignet.org: National Association of Blacks in
  Government
http://bsa.od.nih.gov: Black Scientists Association
www.nbaslh.org: The National Black Association for
  Speech-Language and Hearing
www.aabe.org: American Association of Blacks in

Engineering
www.nabcj.org: National Association of Blacks in Criminal Justice
www.tabphe.org: Texas Association of Blacks in Higher Education
www.nanbpwc.org: National Association of Negro Business and Professional Women's Clubs, Inc.
www.www.namcline.org: National Association of Minority Contractors
www.www.bcasports.org: Black Coaches Association
www.blackactuaries.org: International Association of Black Actuaries
www.www.iobse.com: International Association of Black Security Executives
www.dca.net/isas: International Association of African Scientists

About the Author

Chaz Kyser is a journalism instructor at Langston University and a freelance editor. She received a master of science degree in publishing from Pace University in New York, and bachelor's degrees in print journalism and sociology from Texas State University-San Marcos.

How people manage and become successful in their careers has interested Chaz since she first started working at the age of 14 selling popcorn at a $1 movie theater. Of course in time she moved up at the movie theater (to selling tickets) and then on to bigger and better things with the help of a quality education and a good dose of industriousness and luck.

At the age of 21 she became one of the youngest African-Americans in the nation to serve as the managing editor of a black-owned weekly newspaper. While working in this position and struggling with life after college the idea for a career guide for black female college graduates came to her. However, she had to wait until she had more career and real life experiences to publish it. Those experiences soon came through more than a dozen jobs, four jobs losses, a move across the U.S. and back, an engagement, a broken engagement, feeling secure with lots of money in the bank, negative account balances, dealing with depression from not knowing what she was going to do with her life, and navigating the path that led her to a career she loves.

She has discovered that the real world—the working world—is not to be feared, put off or ignored; it should be embraced. This book is filled with information that has helped Chaz and countless other black women navigate their lives after college.

She hopes it will help you move more confidently in yours, as well motivate you to have the rewarding career and life you deserve.

You may contact Chaz Kyser via email at info@embracingtherealworld.com

Order More Books

Embracing the Real World: The Black Woman's Guide to Life After College can be purchased for $14.99 through the website www.embracingtherealworld.com. Credit cards, money orders, purchase orders and checks are accepted. You can also order the guide from your favorite bookstore. *Embracing the Real World* is an excellent gift for college undergraduates, recent grads, and any savvy and sophisticated young black woman in today's workforce. It can also be used as required or supplemental reading material in classes or for book clubs. Visit the website for discount information on bulk orders.

Notes

Notes

Notes

Notes